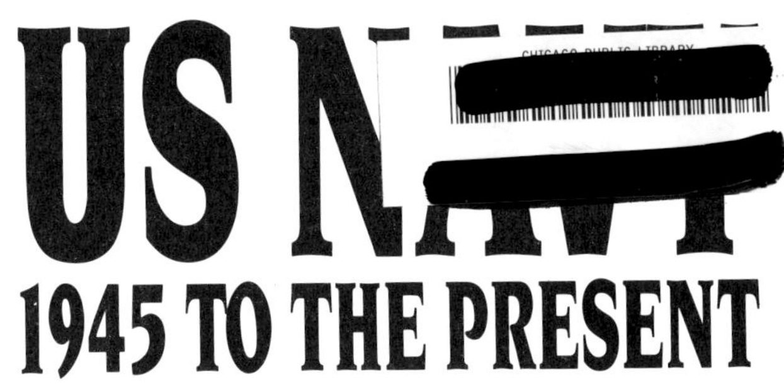

Cover illustrations: front, the *Fletcher* class destroyer *Jarvis*; back top, USS *Trathen*; back bottom, the battleship *Iowa*.

1. The aircraft carrier *Midway* (CVB 41) was completed just after the end of the war. At the time, she was the largest carrier built; only the Japanese *Shinano* (sunk) exceeded her in size. The class was a completely new design with improved underwater protection and armoured sides and deck. Three ships were completed, and they were the first American warships to be too broad to pass through the Panama Canal. In September 1947, an experimental V-2 rocket was launched from Midway's deck.

The distinctive island with large funnel and tripod mast was unmistakable. Ranged along both sides were eighteen 5in guns in single turrets and 84 40mm AA guns. Four of the 5in guns had already been removed when *Midway* cruised in June 1949 with the cruiser *Albany* (CA 123). (USN 426263)

2. Only three ships of the *Oregon City* class were completed, six additional units having been cancelled at the end of the war. They were essentially repeat *Baltimores* with a single large funnel and modified, set-back superstructure. A fourth vessel, *Northampton*, was completed as a command ship. *Oregon City* (CA 122), completed in 1946, shown on her shakedown cruise, was laid up and saw no active service. (USN 262557)

US NAVY
1945 TO THE PRESENT

PAUL SILVERSTONE

ARMS AND
ARMOUR

Arms and Armour Press
A Cassell Imprint
Villiers House, 41–47 Strand,
London WC2N 5JE.

Distributed in the USA by Sterling Publishing Co. Inc., 387 Park Avenue South, New York, NY 10016–8810.

Distributed in Australia by Capricorn Link (Australia) Pty. Ltd, P.O. Box 665, Lane Cove, New South Wales 2066.

Designed and edited by DAG Publications Ltd. Designed by David Gibbons; edited by Michael Boxall; layout by Anthony A. Evans; typeset by Ronset Typesetters Ltd, Darwen, Lancashire; camerawork by M&E Reproductions, North Fambridge, Essex; printed and bound in Great Britain by The Alden Press, Oxford.

British Library Cataloguing in Publication Data
Silverstone, Paul H. (Paul Harold)
1931–
US Navy 1945 to the present.
I. United States. Navy, history
I. Title
359.00973
ISBN 1-85368-921-0

1946

3. The Second World War ended with the opening of the nuclear age. In July 1946 the navy staged two dramatic tests, exploding atomic bombs to determine their effect upon ships and other targets. A fleet of obsolete and surplus ships was collected for use as targets in Operation 'Crossroads'. They included the battleships *Pennsylvania*, *Nevada* and *New York*, carrier *Saratoga*, cruisers *Pensacola* and *Salt Lake City*, destroyers, as well as the former Japanese battleship *Nagato* and German cruiser *Prinz Eugen*. Transports of the target fleet wait at Pearl Harbor in early 1946; *Crittenden* (APA 77), *Catron* (APA 71), and *Bracken* (APA 64) are in the foreground. (NA 80-G-702126)

4. The tests took place at the isolated Pacific atoll of Bikini in the Marshall Islands. The native population was evacuated before the tests began. The first explosion was an air burst which took place on 1 July 1946. Test Baker, three weeks later on 25 July, was an underwater burst which hurled a massive column of water hundreds of feet into the air. The battleship *Nagato* can be seen at right of the base of the column with other ships of the target fleet. (NA 80-G-396228)

Introduction

In 1945 at the end of the Second World War, the United States Navy was not only the largest in its history but also the largest navy that had ever been. More ships and more powerful ships in their hundreds could be seen in every part of the world. In addition newer ships were still on the ways and in the outfitting yards.

The change to a peacetime navy came in 1946. Many ships on order had been cancelled and only a comparative few remained to be completed, to designs modified by wartime experience. Gallant old veterans and some not so old were consigned to the scrapyard. Hundreds of new and usable ships were laid up in back waters where it was expected they would remain until scrapped sometime in the future.

The beginning of the nuclear age which had dawned in the fiery disintegration of Hiroshima and Nagasaki required tests and experiments for both development and protection, and some of the navy's best-known fighting ships were among those saved from the breakers to serve as guinea-pigs in the nuclear tests at Bikini in July 1946.

A major change took place in 1947 with the unification of the armed forces and the establishment of the Department of Defense, incorporating the formerly separate army, navy and air force.

But the United States did not return to the quiet peacetime of the pre-war period. Antagonism with the Soviet Union and its expansionist policies in Europe and Asia became the Cold War in the late 1940s, blossoming into a hot war in Korea in 1950. The navy reactivated many of its laid-up ships and found itself in a real fight once again. Carrier strikes, shore bombardments, amphibious operations and minesweeping were the navy's principal duties during the three years of war in Korea and some ships were sunk and damaged. American forces suffered 54,246 killed or injured during this war.

The 1950s were marked by interesting developments in naval science, new weapons, new ships, electronics and new propulsion. Rapid strides were made in undersea warfare, using the new discoveries made by the Germans during the Second World War such as the snorkel and streamlined hulls, as well as American experience in the Pacific. Anti-submarine warfare received a great deal of attention and here too new weapons, such as Weapon A and new sonar, were made operational.

Initial experiments with guided weapons led by 1957 to shipboard installations of early types of missiles. The destroyer *Gyatt*, fitted with Terrier surface-to-air missiles, was the first guided-missile ship in the navy, soon followed by cruisers converted to that role and later by destroyers and cruisers built for the purpose. The cruiser *Long Beach*, completed in 1961, was the first all-missile-armed cruiser built from the keel up.

Construction of *Long Beach* also marked another first: the first nuclear-powered surface warship. Nuclear propulsion for warships made great strides in the 1950s, initially in submarines. The pioneer submarine *Nautilus*, commissioned in 1955, was so successful that by the 1960s all new submarines built were nuclear-powered. The year 1961 was also marked by the appearance of the aircraft carrier *Enterprise*, the largest warship in the world, powered by eight nuclear reactors. The advantage of nuclear propulsion was that it eliminated the necessity for constant refuelling as well as enabling the ships to make great speed.

As the navy entered the 1960s a new mix of ships and weapons was clearly apparent. Guided missiles, nuclear power and the increasing reliance on electronics and submarines changed the look of the traditional navy.

Congress ordered all new major surface warships to be nuclear powered. Following construction of six cruisers this was found to be counter-productive and too costly and by the late 1970s only the largest aircraft carriers continued to be built with nuclear reactors.

The introduction of the ballistic missile submarine at the beginning of the decade led to the rapid construction of a fleet of large submarines whose principal armament was long-range, pre-targeted missiles with nuclear warheads. Forty-one of these warships were built from 1957 to 1967. All attack submarines were built with nuclear propulsion despite the loss of two of these.

Developments and requirements in amphibious warfare also led to new and larger ships. Amphibious assault ships, combining functions previously allocated to specialized smaller vessels, were designed, carrying assault troops and their equipment and able to deploy them by means of helicopters or landing craft loaded in docking wells. The largest of these eventually were larger than Second World War-type aircraft carriers.

With the Gulf of Tonkin incident, the United States became involved in combat in Vietnam, bringing the navy into battle once again, with carrier strikes, shore bombardment and riverine operations. New types of small craft were developed for use in the shallow and inland waters of Vietnam in a new type of warfare. For almost ten years the war dragged on against increasing opposition at home and when it ended, 57,718 American servicemen had been killed.

At the end of the Vietnam war many older ships were retired because of age, high operating costs or minimal effectiveness. Rising costs for new ships and weapons, the difficulty of recruiting new personnel and a lack of direction in high places led to a reduction in the size of the fleet during the 1970s. Many recommended new programmes were stillborn and only the cruise missile programme and construction of new frigates proceeded as expected. The fleet declined to 476 active ships.

But the Cold War continued and the Soviet Union continued an impressive construction programme, developing for the first time an effective and powerful ocean-going fleet, including aircraft carriers and nuclear-powered cruisers.

The Iranian hostage crisis of 1979–80 was only one of several events which changed the outlook for the navy. A 600-ship navy was envisaged, advanced by Secretary of the Navy John F. Lehman Jr. New nuclear-powered aircraft carriers were authorized, new classes of amphibious ships, the Trident ballistic missile and *Ohio*-class submarines, and reactivation of the four modernized battleships were elements of this plan.

In 1990, following the Iraqi occupation of Kuwait, large elements of the US armed forces were deployed to the Persian Gulf area.

As the navy moves into the 1990s a new direction can be sensed, caused as much by the need to control costs as by the apparent end of the Cold War and a relaxation of tension between the United States and the Soviet Union.

The majority of the pictures used in this book are official US Navy Photographs. The author wishes to thank Ernest Arroyo, Charles Haberlein and Norman Polmar for their assistance with photographs.

5

5. The twenty-four ships of the *Essex* class, built during the war, were the largest class of fleet aircraft carriers ever built and formed the backbone of the post-war navy Here, *Philippine Sea* (CV 47), completed in 1946, lies tied up at Pearl Harbor. At this time they carried five 16-aircraft squadrons, four fighter and one attack.

6. Several ships under construction were left incomplete at the end of the war. One of these was the large cruiser *Hawaii* (CB 3), third ship of the *Alaska* class, launched in 1945 and 82.4 per cent complete when construction was suspended in February 1947. Her superstructure and main battery were already installed and in this view, looking forward, the aft 12in turret can be seen. Conversion to a missile ship was planned but never carried out and the unfinished ship was scrapped in 1958. The other two vessels of the class completed, *Alaska* and *Guam*, were laid up in 1946 and scrapped in 1960. (NH 93585)

7

8

545

9

7. The only battleships remaining in the active fleet after the war were the four *Iowa* class. With a high length to beam ratio, they were the fastest battleships ever built. Their beam was restricted to under 110 feet so that they could transit the Panama Canal. During the Second World War they were superlative escorts for the fast carrier task forces with their great number of AA guns. Here *Missouri* (BB 64) is anchored in New York's Hudson River in April 1946. She later received a tripod in place of the pole mainmast, and the catapult on the stern was removed. In January 1950 she ran aground in Hampton Roads and remained stuck for six days before she was pulled free. All were recommissioned for service in Korea.

8. 150 *Fletcher*-class destroyers remained on the list after the war. This was the first class of destroyers designed after the end of the limitations imposed by the London Treaty of 1930. Larger than previous destroyers, they incorporated increased anti-aircraft armament without reducing either the five 5in guns or the ten torpedo tubes. *Bradford* (DD 545), seen after reactivation in 1950, carries the standard armament of five 5in guns in single turrets and one bank of five torpedo tubes. She has been refitted with a tripod mast to carry the heavier radar installation.

9. There were also 53 surviving units of the larger *Allen M. Sumner* class. *Taussig* (DD 746) retained the original pole mast and numerous anti-aircraft guns. Their 5in guns were carried in twin mounts, and they had a single bank of torpedo tubes between the stacks. Four of this class became war losses and three others were scrapped because of war damage.

1947

10. The ultimate American cruiser design, *Des Moines* (CA 134), was an expanded *Oregon City* with fully automatic rapid-firing 8in gun mounts. Their rate of fire was four times faster than previous guns. The additional weight and size was taken up by the new turrets and the longer waterline armour belt. Only three ships of the class were completed, five being cancelled. This aerial view of *Des Moines* on builder's trials in 1948 shows the general layout of the superstructure and armament. Many of the AA guns were removed soon after commissioning together with the catapults on the stern. (USN 417084)

11. Twenty-seven light cruisers of the *Cleveland* class were completed from 1942 to 1946, and eleven of them served in the active fleet after the Second World War. This picture shows *Dayton* (CL 105), a later unit of the class, serving with the Mediterranean Fleet in 1948. She was laid up in 1949 and scrapped in 1963. (Marius Bar)

12. The second *Juneau* (CL 119) was one of three sisters completed after the war, similar to the *Atlanta–Oakland* classes, the smallest cruisers built by the navy during the war. Although designed as anti-aircraft vessels they were deficient in having only two directors, which restricted the number of aircraft that could be engaged with controlled fire. In addition, as a result of their small size their cruising radius was restricted making them poor as destroyer leaders. Two ships, *Atlanta* and the first *Juneau*, were lost during the war. CL 119 served in Korea and was the last to remain, being decommissioned in 1955.

13. The *Baltimore* class was the standard heavy cruiser design of the Second World War and most of the fourteen units served actively after the war. With their nine 8in guns they were especially effective for shore bombardment in Korea and Vietnam. This is *Bremerton* (CA 130) as she appeared in 1955, with catapults removed from the fantail. (USN 669192)

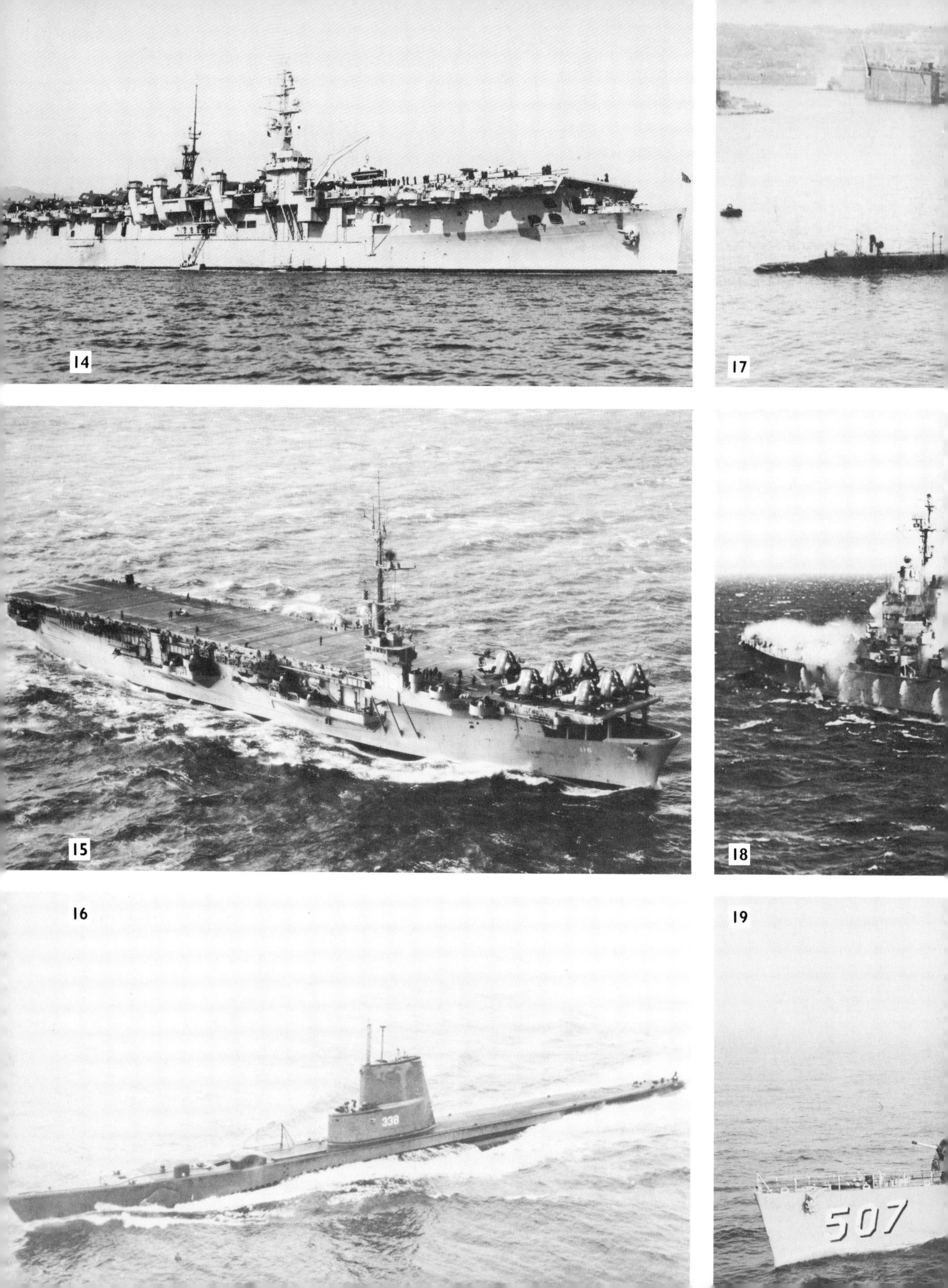
14
17
15
18
16
19
338
507

14. Too small to serve as first-line carriers when completed in 1947, *Saipan* and *Wright* (CVL 49) (above) were used for experimental and anti-submarine duties. The forward (fourth) funnel was removed in 1950. Their hull and machinery duplicate those of the *Baltimore* class heavy cruisers. (Marius Bar)

15. The *Commencement Bay* class was the final development of the escort carrier. Their hulls were similar to the successful converted oilers of the *Sangamon* class. Aircraft capacity was increased to 34. They operated with anti-submarine and composite squadrons. Nineteen ships were completed but two of these, *Rabaul* and *Tinian*, were laid up on delivery and were never used. In 1948, *Badoeng Strait* (CVE 116) (above), *Sicily* and *Mindoro* were equipped with ASW squadrons. Seen here in 1954 with Corsair fighters on the flight deck. (USN 442515)

16. The highly successful *Gato* class numbered 192 units completed between 1941 and 1945. They were the mainstay of the submarine fleet which devastated the Japanese Navy and merchant marine during the Second World War. Twenty-nine became war losses. This was the final pre-war design based on experience gained from vessels constructed during the 1930s. The first modifications made after the war involved streamlining the conning tower, and enclosing the periscopes and snorkel which could be raised for use, as shown here in *Carp* (SS 338). The hull was unchanged but deck guns were removed. The snorkel, developed by the Germans during the war, was a breathing device which allowed the submarine to operate its diesel engines when submerged.

17. Some were modified experimentally for special functions. One of the more successful adaptations was as radar picket. *Requin* (SSR 481), entering Grand Harbour, Malta in 1953, has radar mounted on the conning tower.

1948

18. The cruiser *Worcester* (CL 144) during atomic defence manoeuvres in July 1954. The salt water spraying was supposed to cleanse the ship of radioactive debris. The large light cruisers of the *Worcester* class, completed in 1948–9, were similar in appearance to the *Atlanta* class, with their main armament of twelve 6in guns in six twin mounts. The guns were fully automatic and the ships had greatly improved directed AA firing. Two were completed and two were cancelled in 1945. (USN 709227)

19. Eighteen *Fletcher* class destroyers were converted to escort destroyers during 1948–50, retaining only two 5in guns with two 3in guns and four fixed ASW tubes. Eight carried Weapon A in position two, such as *Conway* (DDE 507), seen here coming alongside the carrier *Randolph* for refuelling. The others had hedgehog devices which fired depth-charges in a pattern. Six later conversions had a tripod foremast in place of *Conway*'s pole.

20. The numerous *Gearing* class, of which 98 were completed, provided the destroyer force of the fleet during the immediate post-war years. They were similar to the earlier *Sumner* class with a 14-foot section added amidships to provide increased space in the hull. Originally planned with two banks of five torpedo tubes, most were completed with only one. A typical unit was *Wiltsie* (DD 716) seen here in 1961 in the Pacific, after refitting with tripod foremast.

21. Thirty-six *Gearing*-class destroyers were fitted with early warning radar, a modification conceived during the Okinawa campaign. Most, like *Hawkins* (DDR 873), were given a tripod mainmast in place of the torpedo tubes, although some units retained one mount. Eight, fitted with TACAN (Tactical Air Navigation System) in 1957, had a smaller tripod mainmast.

22. A *Gearing*-class variant, *Robert A. Owens* (DDE 827), was completed as a hunter-killer (DDK) with two Weapon A rocket-launchers mounted forward and aft and six 3in guns. The ship is shown here in 1958 after being re-armed with two new 3in mounts.

23. *Rich* (DDE 820) was one of four *Gearing*-class units converted to escort destroyers with a hedgehog forward in place of number two 5in mount. She carries a tripod foremast and light mainmast and retains her torpedo tubes.

24. Designed to operate long-range bombers, the supercarrier *United States* (CVA 59) was laid down on 18 April 1949 at Newport News. Four days later she was cancelled, when the Air Force won its fight to operate strategic nuclear attack forces. The flush-deck carrier would have been the largest ship ever built. The dispute over strategic nuclear forces involved all three military services, each competing for a piece of the action. (80-G-707176)

25. The old battleship *Pennsylvania* (BB 38) slips beneath the waves off Kwajalein on 10 February 1948. The former flagship of the US Fleet, and later an atomic target ship at Bikini, was scuttled because of lingering radioactivity. She appears relatively undamaged by the atomic blasts; X turret is swung out to port. (80-G-705028)

26. Another Bikini target ship, the cruiser *Salt Lake City* (CA 25) was sunk as a target in June 1948. A great deal of damage is visible topside and both funnels are missing from this gallant veteran of the Pacific campaigns. (80-G-395404)

27. A GUPPY conversion (Greater Underwater Propulsive Power), *Grampus* (SS 523) shows the new look in this 1957 view. Altogether 48 submarines of the *Gato* and *Tench* classes were rebuilt, with streamlined contours, rounded bows, smooth conning towers with periscopes, radar and snorkel enclosed in a tower. Shape of the conning towers varied. The snorkel breathing device which enabled the submarine to remain submerged without surfacing to replenish air was developed from captured German devices. One GUPPY conversion, *Cochino* (SS 345), was lost off the northern coast of Norway on 26 August 1949.

25

26

27

1949

28. Three small experimental hunter-killer submarines were ordered in 1948–9. It was intended that they would be mass produced in time of war. Originally known only as K-1 to K-3, they were given 'B' names in 1955. K-1 (SSK 1) became *Barracuda* and was converted for training in 1959; the large sonar dome in the bow was removed.

29. Three Coast Guard icebreakers lent to the Soviet Union in 1944 under Lend-Lease were returned in 1949. *Atka* (AGB 3) was commissioned in the navy in 1950, and was returned to the Coast Guard in 1966 when she resumed her former name *Southwind*. The helicopter landing deck was added in the 1950s. Seven 'Wind'-class icebreakers were built, the two Navy ships joining their five Coast Guard sisters in 1967.

30

31

30. The four ships of the *Mitscher* class ordered in 1948 were the first post-war destroyer-type vessels. They were designed as fast ocean escorts, completing in 1953–4 as frigates, but their machinery was unreliable. All were named after famous admirals of the Second World War. On completion they were armed with two 5in and four 3in guns, Weapon A rocket-launcher and four torpedo tubes. The mixed battery of single 5in and twin 3in mounts is noticeable in *Wilkinson* (DL 5) in this 1956 picture. (USN)

1950

31. Forty-one *Fletcher*-class destroyers were modified during the 1950s, losing their number three 5in gun mount. A tripod foremast was fitted and two twin 3in gun mountings were added amidships. *Caperton* (DD 650) was a typical unit, shown under way at sea in October 1953. (USN 631323)

32. In 1950 the light carriers *Bataan* and *Cabot* were refitted for anti-submarine warfare, with decks reinforced to operate heavier aircraft. *Bataan* (CVL 29), seen here at sea in 1952, lost two funnels in the process. She served in the Korean War before laying up in 1954. The class of nine was converted from *Cleveland*-class light cruisers while under construction as a stopgap measure to relieve the shortage of carriers in 1942. They served as firstline units in the Pacific with the fast carrier task forces. (USN 633888)

33. Four aluminium-hulled motor torpedo-boats were built in 1950 to take advantage of wartime experience. With four Packard gasoline engines, they were rated at 42 knots. All were stricken in 1959, but *PT-810* (above) and *PT-811* were reinstated in 1962 as *PTF 1–2* and later served in Vietnam.

33

34. Destroyers *Sarsfield* (DD 837) and *Epperson* (DDE 719) carry out anti-submarine manoeuvres using hedgehog off Key West in 1950. The characteristic circular pattern results from a launcher firing a pattern of depth-charges ahead of the ship.

35. Although launched in 1945, completion of the carrier *Oriskany* (CV 34) was delayed in order to incorporate wartime lessons. She was commissioned in October 1950 with stronger decks and a smaller island to enable her to carry heavier jet aircraft. Anti-aircraft guns line the sides of the flight deck.

36. The incomplete hull of the battleship *Kentucky* (BB 66) is moved in February 1950 to make room for *Missouri*, damaged by grounding. Suspended at the end of the war, she was launched to vacate the slip in 1950. The hull was completed only to the main deck with machinery installed; two of the barbettes can be seen. Various plans were proposed to convert her to a missile ship but nothing came of these and she was scrapped in 1958. (80-G-413973)

37. In June 1950 war broke out in Korea and US armed forces went into action under the flag of the United Nations. North Korean armies were initially successful, occupying all of the south except a small perimeter around Pusan. The first major amphibious operation since the end of the Second World War took place at Inchon, 15 September 1950, to break the stalemate at Pusan. Supporting bombardment began on the 13th, but because of the extreme tides in Inchon Bay ships had to withdraw each time the tide ebbed. Initial landings were made on the island of Wolmi-Do. The city of Inchon fell on the 16th, Marine aircraft began using Kimpo airfield for operations on the 21st and Seoul, the capital, was captured on the 24th. Four LSTs are seen unloading men and equipment on the beach on 15 September.

38. Further landings were planned to be made at Wonsan on the west coast, but by the date of the operation the enemy had withdrawn and the landing was unopposed. Six American and Korean LSTs unload in Wonsan harbour, 26 October 1950, following landing by the 1st Marine Division.

39. The heavy cruiser *Helena* (CA 75) bombarding North Korean shore positions at Chong Ji, October 1950, in support of the Wonsan landings.

34

35

36

37

38

39

40. Koreans prepare to board an LST during the evacuation from Hungnam in December 1950. In addition to military personnel, thousands of civilians were helped to flee from North Korean forces which reoccupied the port. Following the success of the Inchon landings, United Nations forces crossed the demarcation line into North Korea and pushed further north to the Yalu River boundary with China. This brought armies of the People's Republic of China into Korea, leading to the loss of almost all the North Korean territory which had been occupied.

41. *Bayonne* (PF 21) was one of twelve frigates hastily recommissioned for service in Korea during 1950–3. They were part of a group of twenty-seven returned by the Soviet Union in 1949 under wartime Lend-Lease arrangements. The twenty-eighth, *Belfast*, was lost in 1948 while in Russian hands. These were similar to the British *River* class but with heavier armament. Eventually all the returned ships were transferred to foreign navies.

44

45

1951

42. A Sikorski HO3S-1 helicopter lands on the aircraft carrier *Boxer* (CV 21) during air-sea rescue operations off Korea, 13 September 1951.

43. The minesweeper *Mocking Bird* (AMS 27) explodes an enemy mine in the Yellow Sea off Chinnampo. During the war several South Korean ships and three American minesweepers were sunk while engaged in mine warfare operations.

44. The big guns of the battleship *Wisconsin* (BB 64) firing a salvo at North Korean positions, 30 January 1952.

45. As part of the early warning detection system, 34 diesel-engined destroyer escorts received a major conversion from 1950 to 1956, with a built-up deckhouse amidships, tripod masts and radar. *Harveson* (DER 316) was one of the first to be converted. Together with converted Liberty ships (AGR) and aircraft, they reported unidentified aircraft to Continental Air Defense (CONAD) headquarters at Colorado Springs.

46. The battleship *Missouri* (BB 63) ties up at Norfolk on her return from Korea, 27 April 1951. Alongside, making an interesting contrast in size, are the heavy cruisers *Macon* (CA 132) and *Albany* (CA 123). (USN 428357)

1952

47. While conducting manoeuvres west of the Azores on 26 April 1952, the destroyer/minesweeper *Hobson* (DMS 26) ran in front of the aircraft carrier *Wasp* (CV 18) and was sliced in two, sinking with a loss of 176 men. *Jeffers* (DMS 27), a sister ship, shown under way in 1951, was one of 24 destroyers of the *Livermore* class converted in 1944–5 losing their torpedo tubes and after 5in gun mount to minesweeping equipment. Four were lost during the war and many of the rest remained in service during the following decade, the last being decommissioned in 1956. (USN 479910)

46

48

47

49

48. The battleship *Iowa* (BB 61) followed by *New Jersey* (BB 62) during the early 1950s. A tripod structure has been fitted on the after funnel. The spectacle of two battleships at sea together would not be seen again until 1984.

49. *Lake Champlain* (CV 39) was one of the *Essex* class never converted to an angled flight deck. She was modernized in 1952 with a modified island structure and new deck-edge elevator.

50. *Antietam* (CV 36) received an experimental, angled flight deck in 1952, an innovation continued in all future carriers and incorporated into major refits of many sister ships. The carrier is seen here under way in Gravesend Bay, New York following its installation on 5 January 1953. (80-G-478412)

51

51. Between 1952 and 1954 twelve destroyer escorts were lent to the Coast Guard. They were painted white and used numbers in the 400 series prefixed with 'W'. This is *Durant* (WDE 489, ex-DE 389) as a Coast Guard ship. She was later converted to a radar picket ship.

52. *Trout* (SS 566) shows the original appearance of the first post-war submarines, the six fast attack boats of the *Tang* class. Completed in 1952, their design incorporated features of the German Type XXI including hull form, superstructure and snorkel. The first four had radial diesel engines but were rebuilt with new engines and lengthened in 1957. (USN 447521)

1953

53. The revolutionary new teardrop-shaped hull form made its first appearance in 1953 in the experimental submarine *Albacore* (AGSS 569). When completed she was the fastest submarine afloat, being able to make 33 knots submerged. The hull form was incorporated into all nuclear submarines after 1955 starting with the *Skipjack* class. *Albacore* was modified several times after completion in order to test new equipment. (USN 636615)

54

54. The experimental hunter-killer ship N*orfolk* (DL 1) was designed in 1948 as a cruiser-type anti-submarine vessel (CLK), but proved too expensive for an ASW unit. Eventually reclassified as a frigate, she was commissioned in 1953. Construction of a second vessel was deferred in 1949. Her original armament consisted of eight 3in guns in twin mounts, four Weapon A launchers and two quadruple torpedo tube mounts. A distinctive vessel with clipper bow and stacks of unequal height, she had two six-bladed propellers. In 1955 she was the primary test ship for the anti-submarine weapon ASROC. (USN 1024239)

55. The tactical command ship *Northampton* (CLC 1) was begun as a heavy cruiser of the *Oregon City* class. Construction was halted in 1945 when 56.2 per cent complete; the vessel was reordered in 1948 to a new design. Built a deck higher than her sisters, her forward guns are off centre to clear the foremast on the bow. She is seen here after her 1961 conversion to serve as National Emergency Command Post Afloat (NECPA). The storeship *Alstede* (AF 48) is alongside.

56. The cluttered after deck of the non-magnetic wooden-hulled minesweeper *Observer* (MSO 461) shows paravanes and cable drums. Ninety-seven vessels of the *Agile* class were built of which 35 went to other NATO countries. The minesweeper building programme was begun in response to the extensive use of mines in the Korean War. The diesel engines were made of stainless steel alloy, and metal fittings of aluminium or brass. Modernization of the class, including new engines and advanced sweeping gear, was cancelled in 1968 when minesweeping duties were allocated to helicopters and only nineteen of the class were actually refitted.

57. Two Liberty ships were acquired in 1953 to investigate and test for fallout following nuclear tests. *Granville S. Hall* (YAG 40) was fitted with a helicopter deck forward. She was stricken in 1967.

1954

58. The old battleship *Mississippi* (AG 128), built in 1917, was retained after the war, originally as a gunnery training ship and later for testing missiles. In August 1953, the first successful firing of Terrier SAM occurred; here (1954) a Terrier missile is being fired. Notice the tripod mainmast and other missiles ready for firing. (80-G-K-17878)

59. A new class of Dock Landing Ships was built during the early 1950s, the eight ships of the *Thomaston* class. Similar to the wartime *Ashland* class, the stern section consists of a dock in which loaded landing craft can be carried which can then proceed under their own power from the dock when flooded. *Fort Snelling* (LSD 30) can carry three LCUs or nine LCMs. Her original armament included sixteen 3in guns, gradually reduced during the years.

60

61

62

1955

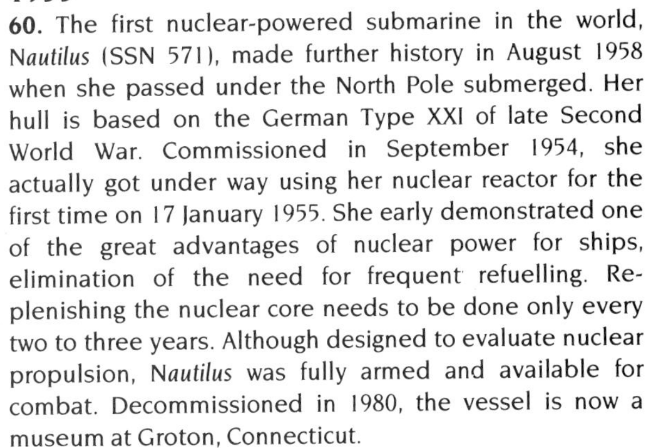

60. The first nuclear-powered submarine in the world, *Nautilus* (SSN 571), made further history in August 1958 when she passed under the North Pole submerged. Her hull is based on the German Type XXI of late Second World War. Commissioned in September 1954, she actually got under way using her nuclear reactor for the first time on 17 January 1955. She early demonstrated one of the great advantages of nuclear power for ships, elimination of the need for frequent refuelling. Replenishing the nuclear core needs to be done only every two to three years. Although designed to evaluate nuclear propulsion, *Nautilus* was fully armed and available for combat. Decommissioned in 1980, the vessel is now a museum at Groton, Connecticut.

61. *Hull* (DD 945) was a typical unit of the *Forrest Sherman* class, the first class of destroyers designed and built after the Second World War. Eighteen ships were built from 1953 to 1959 and remained in service until 1982. She carries a single 5in and twin 3in mounts forward, and two 5in mounts aft.

62. As part of the early warning system set up in the 1950s, sixteen Liberty ships were converted to radar pickets to cover the seaward approaches. They remained in service until 1965. The familiar Liberty profile of *Locator* (AGR 6) is clearly visible despite the addition of heavy masts to support the radars.

63. The escort carrier *Corregidor* (T-CVU 58) as a utility carrier or aircraft transport in 1957. Two cranes have been erected on the deck and there are two small smokepipes on the starboard side. (USN 1029689)

64. LSMR-527, later named *St. Joseph River*, was one of 48 medium landing ships converted to rocket landing ships and given 'River' names in 1955. They carried a single 5in gun with eight or ten twin rocket-launchers, able to fire thirty rounds per minute. Several were recommissioned for service in Vietnam in 1965. (USN 1045570)

65. An improved rocket landing ship, the inshore fire support ship *Carronade* (IFS 1) was a prototype, improved LSMR commissioned in 1955. No others of this type were built. She was considerably larger than the LSMRs but similarly armed. Laid up in 1960, she was reactivated for service in Vietnam in 1970.

66

66. The first 'supercarrier', *Forrestal* was completed in 1955 as an attack carrier. This picture shows the last of the class of four, *Independence* (CVA 62), in 1962, operating with *Enterprise* in the Caribbean. The increasing size of aircraft necessitated larger carriers. The hangar deck is 25 feet high as contrasted to 17½ feet in *Midway*. During construction the design was modified to include an angled flight deck. Many of the new features included were derived from the cancelled *United States* of 1948. An A-4 Skyhawk aircraft is being launched and a Sea Knight helicopter approaches from starboard.

67. The cruiser *Canberra* (CAG 2) was one of the first two ships to include guided missiles as part of their main armament. Former *Baltimore*-class vessels, she and her sister, *Boston*, had their after gun turret replaced by two twin launchers for Terrier SAMs, the superstructure modified and the twin funnels replaced by a single stack. The magazine could hold 144 missiles. Earlier, *Helena*, *Los Angeles*, *Macon* and *Toledo* had been fitted with Regulus missiles using the aircraft hangars to house them. In 1968 *Boston* and *Canberra* were reclassified as heavy cruisers after the decision was made not to modernize them.

1956

68. In 1956 the escort carrier *Thetis Bay* (LPH 6) was converted to an amphibious assault ship at San Francisco Naval Shipyard. She was built originally as one of 50 escort carriers of the *Casablanca* class. Her classification was changed from CVHA 1 to LPH in 1959.

69. The aircraft carrier *Franklin* D. *Roosevelt* (CVA 42) following her 1956 refit during which she received angled flight deck and steam catapults. Notice the conical heavy foremast and 5in guns on the side. Her deck is crowded with several types of aircraft and helicopters. *Roosevelt* was decommissioned in 1977 and scrapped after 32 years of continuous service.

68

69

70. The two radar picket boats ordered in 1952 were the largest non-nuclear submarines built for the navy since the *Narwhal* class of 1928. Like *Sailfish* (SSR 572), they had a large radar antenna behind the sail and a second inside it. In 1961 they were converted to attack submarines and the radars were removed. (USN 10329)

71. The conventionally powered submarine *Darter* (SS 576), another single unit, completed in 1956, was an improvement of the *Tang* class. (USN 1002794)

72. *Kearsarge* (CVS 33) was one of fourteen *Essex*-class carriers to receive the full conversion treatment of angled flight deck, enclosed bow, modified island with new radar masts and new deck-edge elevators. Seen here at sea in 1962 with TF-1 Trader twin-engined aircraft on deck.

70

71

72

1957

73. *Seawolf* (SSN 575) was the second nuclear-powered submarine, built with a sodium-cooled reactor as a competitive prototype with *Nautilus*. After two years it was replaced with a reactor similar to that in *Nautilus*, when this picture was taken. Completed in 1957, *Seawolf* was engaged in research activities from 1969 until being decommissioned in 1987. (General Dynamics)

74. *MacDonough* (DLG 8, later DDG 39), seen here at Malta in 1967, was one of ten guided missile frigates of the *Coontz* class built between 1957 and 1960. They had one twin launcher for Terrier missiles aft, a single 5in gun and ASROC launcher forward. In 1975 they were reclassified as missile destroyers (DDG). (Pavia)

75. *Swordfish* (SSN 579) entering San Francisco Bay, passes Alcatraz Island. She was one of four boats of the *Skate* class, the first production model nuclear submarines. Although smaller than *Nautilus* they carried eight 21in torpedo tubes. Completed 1957–9, they were phased out of service between 1983 and 1988.

76

77

1958

76. Locked in fatal embrace; the submarine *Stickleback* (SS 415) is impaled on the bows of the escort *Silverstein* (DE 534) following a collision off Hawaii on 25 May 1958 while engaged in anti-submarine manoeuvres. The submarine sank before she could be towed back to port. (USN 1036229)

77. The seaplane tender *Albemarle* (AV 5) was reactivated in 1957 to service the Seamaster, a four-jet minelaying seaplane, production of which was cancelled in 1959. Here a P5M Marlin rests on her service deck. She was later converted to a helicopter repair ship and renamed *Corpus Christie Bay* (ARVH 1) to support army helicopters in Vietnam.

78. The tank landing ship *King County* (AG 157) was used as a test ship for the Regulus II missile in 1958. A surface-to-surface missile, Regulus II was 57 feet long with a range of 1,000 miles and nuclear-capable. The Regulus programme was discontinued in December 1958.

79. The submarine *Grayback* (SSG 574) with a Regulus I cruise missile poised for launch. *Grayback* and *Growler* were originally ordered as diesel-powered *Darter*-class attack submarines, but reordered as guided-missile submarines. They were designed to carry two Regulus II cruise missiles. When the Regulus programme was cancelled in 1958, they nevertheless made nine patrols in the western Pacific between 1959 and 1964 with Regulus I missiles. In 1964 *Grayback* was converted to a transport submarine with the missile hangars used as chambers for swimmers and their vehicles, but conversion of *Growler* was cancelled because of increased cost.

80. The first launch of the Regulus II missile from a submarine took place on 17 September 1958 from the guided-missile submarine *Grayback* (SSG 574). (USN 1037783)

78

79

80

81

82

83

84

81. From 1956 to 1960, six *Cleveland*-class cruisers were converted to guided-missile ships. They were partial conversions only, retaining one or two 6in turrets forward. *Oklahoma City* (CLG 5) was fitted with one Talos SAM launcher aft. The forward superstructure was enlarged to make space for flag accommodations which necessitated removal of the number two 6in turret. Notice the high trellis mainmast and extensive missile controls aft.

82. *Galveston* (CLG 3), seen here at Malta in 1968, retained two turrets forward and was also Talos equipped. Laid up on completion in 1946, she was first commissioned in 1958 after conversion to a guided-missile cruiser.

83. The missile cruiser *Little Rock* (CLG 4) firing a Talos surface-to-air missile. Talos was a two-stage solid-fuel rocket with nuclear or conventional warhead and a range of about 75 miles. It was phased out in the late 1970s.

84. *Springfield* (CLG 7) had a different conversion with a single Terrier launcher aft and retaining only one 6in turret forward. She has three masts as well as the Terrier directors aft. Terrier was a nuclear-capable anti-aircraft missile since replaced by the Standard-ER SAM.

85

86

87

1959

85. When completed in 1959, *Triton* (SSRN 586) was the longest US submarine built. Constructed as a radar-picket to provide early warning of air attack on a carrier task force, she was reclassified as an attack submarine in 1961, with the end of the radar picket programme. The retractable radar antenna was housed in the large sail. Until 1973, *Triton* was the only submarine with two nuclear reactors. In May 1960 she completed an underwater circumnavigation of the world. She was decommissioned in 1969, never having served operationally as a radar-picket and was unsuccessful as an attack submarine.

86. In March 1959, *Skate* (SSN 578) became the first submarine to surface at the North Pole. During the cruise she surfaced through the ice pack ten times. (USN 1040961)

87. *Skipjack* (SSN 585), name ship of her class, which was unique in several aspects. They were the first to have the high-speed 'teardrop' hull developed in the experimental *Albacore*, had only one propeller and mounted their diving planes on the sail. They were the fastest submarines of their time, able to make more than 30 knots underwater. Built in 1956–61, they were decommissioned in 1986–7.

88. *Boxer* (CVS 21), an anti-submarine warfare carrier, in 1959 with helicopters on deck. She retained her original basic appearance with axial flight deck and 5in gun mounts. In 1959 she was converted to an amphibious assault ship and was scrapped in 1971. (USN 1040375)

89. *John R. Perry* (DE 1034) was one of four frigates of the *Claud Jones* class, which were too lightly armed and considered a failure. Built in 1957–9, they were sold to Indonesia in 1973–4. They had a chunky appearance and were armed with only two 3in guns and anti-submarine weapons. They had diesel engines and were to have controls for DASH, a programme later cancelled. (VC-1-33175-3-67)

90. Helicopters poised on the specially marked deck of *Princeton* (LPH 5) after her conversion to an amphibious assault ship. Three carriers which had not received angled flight decks were converted pending completion of the *Iwo Jima* class. Others were *Valley Forge* and *Boxer*. Notice the prominent port deck-edge elevator.

1960

91. *Robert E. Lee* (SSBN 601), one of the *George Washington* class, the first class of submarines in the West to be armed with ballistic missiles. Authorized in 1958 they were rushed to completion, the first two being completed in just over two years each, having been converted from *Skipjack*-class attack submarines already authorized. They were redesigned by inserting 130 additional feet in the hull aft of the sail to provide space for two rows of eight missile tubes and associated fire control and navigation systems. They carried Polaris A-1 missiles, modified to fire A-3 missiles in 1964. They could not be armed with the Poseidon missile without extensive modifications and were all withdrawn as SSBN in 1980–1. (Newport News)

US Navy: Basic Data 1946–1962

Type	Class	Number built (converted) or on list 1946	First commissioned	Standard displacement (tons)[1]	Full load displacement (tons)[2]	Overall length (ft)	Waterline length (ft)	Beam (ft)	Maximum draft (ft)	Extreme width (ft)[3]	Propellers	Horsepower[4]	Speed (knots)[5]	Machinery[6]	Complement	Aircraft	Armament[7]
AIRCRAFT CARRIERS																	
CV	Essex short	10	1943	27,100	33,000	876	820	93	30	138	4	150,000	33	ST	2,500	80	12×5in/38, 44–52×40mm
CV	Essex long	14	1944	27,100	33,000	888	820	93	30	130	4	150,000	33	ST	2,500	80	12×5in/38, 44–56×40mm
CV	*Antietam*	1	1952	30,000	38,000	888	820	93	31	154	4	150,000	33	ST	3,227	45+	12×5in
CV	*Midway*	3	1945	51,000	62,000	974	900	111	36	210	4	212,000	33	ST	3,000	130	14×5in/54, 84×40mm
CV	*Midway* (56)	3	1945	51,000	62,000	974	900	111	36	210	4	212,000	33	ST	3,300	70+	10×5in
CV	United States	–	(1949)	66,850	78,500	1088	1030	130	34′6	190	4	280,000	33	ST	4,127		8×5in, 16×3in, 2 SAM
CV	*Oriskany*	8	1950	33,100	41,900	899	820	102	31	192	4	150,000	33	ST	2,500+	70+	8×5in
CV	*Forrestal*	1	1955	54,600	76,000	1039	990	130	37	232	4	260,000	34	ST	4,000+	70+	8×5in
CV	*Enterprise*	1	1961	74,700	85,350	1123	1040	133	35′9	248	4	280,000	30+	ST, 8 reactors	4,000+	70+	
CVL	*Cowpens*	5	1943	11,000	15,800	623	600	71′6	26	109	4	100,000	32	ST	1,400+	30+	28×40mm
CVL	*Saipan*	2	1946	14,500	20,000	683′7	664	76′9	25	115	4	120,000	33	ST	1,400	50	40×40mm
CVE	*Bogue*	10	1942	9,800	15,700	495′8	465	69′6	26	112	1	8,500	17.6	GT	890	30	2×5in, 20×40mm
CVE	*Suwannee*	3	1942	12,000	24,275	553	525	75	31	114	2	12,000	19.1	GT	1,066	35	2×5in, 28×40mm
CVE	*Anzio*	34	1943	9,570	10,400	512′3	490	65′2	22′4	108	2	9,000	19.3	recip	860	30	1×5in, 16×40mm
CVE	*Commencement Bay*	19	1944	11,373	24,275	557′1	525	75	32	105	2	12,000	19.1	GT	1,066	35	2×5in, 36×40mm
NUCLEAR SUBMARINES																	
SSBN	*George Washington*	5	1959	6,000	6,700	381′8	–	33	29	–	1	15,000	20/25	ST, 1 reactor	140	–	16 A-3 Polaris, 6×21in TT
SSBN	*Ethan Allen*	5	1961	6,955	7,900	410′6	–	33	30	–	1	15,000	20/25	ST, 1 reactor	140	–	16 A-3 Polaris, 4×21in TT
SSN	*Nautilus*	1	1954	3,530	4,040	319′5	–	27′6	22	–	2	15,000	18/20+	ST, 1 reactor	120	–	6×21in TT
SSN	*Seawolf*	1	1957	3,720	4,280	337′6	–	27′9	22	–	2	15,000	19/20+	ST, 1 reactor	120	–	6×21in TT

Type	Class	Number built (converted) or on list 1946	First commissioned	Standard displacement (tons)[1]	Full load displacement (tons)[2]	Overall length (ft)	Waterline length (ft)	Beam (ft)	Maximum draft (ft)	Extreme width (ft)[3]	Propellers	Horsepower[4]	Speed (knots)[5]	Machinery[6]	Complement	Aircraft	Armament[7]
SSN	*Skate*	4	1957	2,570	2,861	267′7	–	25	21	–	2	7,500	15.5/20+	ST, 1 reactor	108	–	8×21in TT
SSN	*Skipjack*	6	1959	3,075	3,500	251′9	–	31′6	28	–	1	15,000	15/30+	ST, 1 reactor	112	–	6×21in TT
SSN	*Triton*	1	1959	5,940	6,670	447′6	–	37	24	–	2	34,000	27/20+	ST, 1 reactor	159	–	6×21in TT
SSN	*Halibut*	1	1960	3,850	5,000	350	–	29′6	21′6	–	2	7,500	15.5/15+	ST, 1 reactor	120	–	Regulus II, 6×21in TT
DIESEL SUBMARINES																	
SS	*Gato*	161	1941	1,525	2,425	311′9	–	27	17	–	2	4,600/6,400	20/10	D-E	85	–	10×21in TT, 1×5in
SS	*Tench*	31	1944	1,570	2,500	311′6	–	27′2	17	–	2	4,600/6,400	20/10	D-E	85	–	10×21in TT, 1×5in
SS	*Guppy IA*	10	1951	1,800	2,400	307	–	27	17	–	2	4,610/6,400	20/15	D-E	85	–	10×21in TT
SS	*Guppy II*	15	1951	2,040	2,400	307′6	–	27′4	18	–	2	4,610/6,400	20/15	D-E	85	–	10×21in TT
SS	*Guppy IIA*	16	1951	2,075	2,410	306	–	27	17	–	2	4,800/3,430	18/15	D-E	85	–	10×21in TT
SS	*Guppy III*	9	1951	2,320	2,870	318′10	–	27′3	17	-	2	4,610/6,400	20/15	D-E	84	–	10×21in TT
SSK	*Barracuda*	3	1951	765	1,000	196	–	25	16	–	2	1,050/1,050	13/10	D-E	48	–	4×21in TT
SS	*Tang*	6	1952	1,670	2,110	278	–	27	17	–	2	4,500/3,200	20/17	D-E	83	–	8×21in TT
SS	*Gudgeon (Tang)*	2	1952	1,615	2,000	269	–	27	17	–	2	4,500/4,600	20/17	D-E	83	–	8×21in TT
SST	*Mackerel*	2	1953	250	310	133	–	13′5	12′5	–	1	380/380	10/8.2	D-E	14	–	1×21in TT
AGSS	*Albacore*	1	1953	1,500	1,850	210′6	–	27′4	18′6	–	1	1,500/15,000	25/33	D-E	52	–	none
SS	*Darter*	1	1956	1,620	2,100	268	–	27	19	–	2	4,500/4,500	19.5/14	D-E	85	–	8×21in TT
SSR	*Sailfish*	2	1956	2,030	3,168	350′6	–	29	–	–	2	2,625/3,168	19.5/14	D-E	95	–	6×21in TT
SSG	*Growler*	1	1958	2,540	3,515	317′7	–	27′2	19	–	2	4,600/5,600	20/12+	D-E	88	–	Regulus I, 6×21in TT
SSG	*Grayback*	1	1958	2,670	3,650	334	–	30	19	–	2	4,500/5,600	20/12+	D-E	95	–	Regulus I, 8×21in TT
SS	*Barbel*	3	1959	2,145	2,895	219′6	–	29	28	–	1	4,800/3,150	15/25	D-E	78	–	6×21in TT
BATTLESHIPS																	
BB	*Iowa*	4	1943	45,000	57,540	887′3	860	108′2	38	–	4	212,000	32.5	ST	2,750	–	9×16in, 20×5in, 80×40mm
CRUISERS																	
CB	*Alaska*	2	1944	27,000	34,250	808′6	791′6	91′1	32′4	–	4	150,000	31.4	ST	2,251	–	9×12in, 12×5in, 56×40mm

CL	*Cleveland*	27	1942	10,000	14,400	610'1	600	66'4	25'3	–	4	100,000	31.6	ST	1,285	–	12×6in, 12×5in, 28×40mm
CLAA	*San Diego*	2	1942	6,000	8,600	541'6	530	53'2	26'8	–	2	75,000	31.8	ST	812	–	16×5in, 14×40mm
CLAA	*Oakland*	4	1943	6,000	8,600	541'6	530	53'2	26'8	–	2	75,000	31.8	ST	812	–	12×5in, 24×40mm
CL	*Fargo*	2	1945	10,000	13,350	610	600	66	25	–	4	100,000	33	ST	1,200	–	12×6in, 12×5in, 28×40mm
CLAA	*Juneau*	3	1946	6,000	8,450	541'6	530	53'2	26'8	–	2	75,000	31.8	ST	812	–	12×5in, 14×3in
CA	*Baltimore*	14	1943	13,600	17,200	673'5	664	70'10	26'10	–	4	120,000	32.5	ST	1,775	–	9×8in, 12×5in, 48×40mm
CA	*Oregon City*	3	1946	13,700	17,000	673'6	664	71	26	–	4	120,000	33	ST	1,700	–	9×8in, 12×5in, 52×40mm
CL	*Worcester*	2	1948	14,700	18,500	679'6	668	70'8	25	–	4	120,000	32	ST	1,700	–	12×6in, 20×3in, 12×40mm
CA	*Des Moines*	3	1948	17,000	21,500	716'6	700	75'4	26	–	4	120,000	33	ST	1,860	–	9×8in, 12×5in, 20×3in

GUIDED-MISSILE CRUISERS

CAG	*Boston*	2	1955	13,300	17,500	673'5	664	70'10	29	–	4	120,000	33	ST	1,700	–	2 twin Terrier, 6×8in, 10×5in, 12×3in
CLG	*Galveston*	1	1959	10,500	15,142	610'1	600	66	25	–	4	100,000	32	ST	1,395	–	1 twin Talos, 6×6in, 6×5in
CLG	*Oklahoma City*	2	1959	10,670	14,500	610'1	600	66'4	25	–	4	100,000	32	ST	1,200	–	1 twin Talos, 3×6in, 2×5in
CLG	*Providence*	2	1959	10,670	15,200	610'1	600	66	25'5	–	4	100,000	32	ST	1,145	–	1 twin Terrier, 3×6in, 2×5in
CLG	*Topeka*	1	1960	10,670	14,400	610'1	600	66'6	25	–	4	100,000	32	ST	1,200	–	1 twin Terrier, 6×6in, 6×5in

COMMAND SHIP

CC	*Northampton*	1	1953	12,320	17,200	676	664	71	21	–	4	120,000	32	ST	1,675	–	4×5in, 8×3in

FRIGATES

DL	*Norfolk*	1	1953	5,600	7,300	540'2	520	54'2	26	–	2	80,000	32	ST	600	–	4 Weapon A, 8×3in, 8×21in TT
DL	*Mitscher*	4	1953	3,500	4,730	493	450	50	21	–	2	80,000	35	ST	440	–	Weapon A, 2×5in, 4×3in, 4×21in TT
DL	*Farragut* (=DDG)	10	1959	4,150	5,800	513	490	52'6	23'5	–	2	85,000	33	ST	375	–	1 Terrier, ASROC, 1×5in, 2×3in

Type	Class	Number built (converted) or on list 1946	First commissioned	Standard displacement (tons)[1]	Full load displacement (tons)[2]	Overall length (ft)	Waterline length (ft)	Beam (ft)	Maximum draft (ft)	Extreme width (ft)[3]	Propellers	Horsepower[4]	Speed (knots)[5]	Machinery[6]	Complement	Aircraft	Armament[7]
DESTROYERS																	
DD	*Benson*	27	1940	1,620	2,525	347'10	341	36'1	13'6	–	2	47,000	36.7	ST	276	–	4×5in, 4–12×40mm, 10×21in TT
DD	*Gleaves*	48	1940	1,630	2,525	348'4	341	36'1	13'6	–	2	50,000	36.7	ST	276	–	4×5in, 4–12×40mm, 10×21in TT
DD	*Fletcher*	150	1942	2,050	2,940	376'5	369	39'7	13'9	–	2	60,000	35.2	ST	329	–	5×5in, 10×40mm, 10×21in TT
DDE	*Fletcher*	19	1949	2,050	2,650	376'6	369	39'4	18	–	2	60,000	35	ST	300	–	Weapon A, 2×5in, 5×21in TT
DD	*Fletcher* II	41	1952	2,050	3,040	376'6	369	39'4	18	–	2	60,000	35	ST	300	–	4×5in, 6×3in, 5×21in TT
DD	*Sumner*	53	1944	2,200	3,000	376'6	369	40'10	19	–	2	60,000	34	ST	350	–	6×5in, 12×40mm, 5×21in TT
DD	*Gearing*	96	1944	2,425	3,000	390'6	383	40'10	19	–	2	60,000	35	ST	350	–	6 or 4×5in, 12×40mm, 5×21in TT
DD	*Forrest Sherman*	11	1955	2,780	3,950	418	407	45'2	20	–	2	70,000	33	ST	350	–	3×5in, 4×3in, 4×21in TT
DDG	C. F. *Adams*	23	1960	3,370	4,500	437	420	47	27'3	–	2	70,000	30	ST	354	–	ASROC, 1 twin Tartar, 2×5in, 6×21in TT
ESCORTS (later FRIGATES)																	
DE	*Buckley*/TE	57	1943	1,400	2,170	306	300	36'10	14	–	2	12,000	24	T-E	220	–	3 or 2×3in, 6×40mm, 3×21in TT
DE	*Cannon*/DET	23	1943	1,240	1,900	306	300	36'10	14	–	2	6,000	21	D-E	220	–	3×3in, 2×40mm, 3×21in TT
DE	*Edsall*/FMR	81	1943	1,200	1,850	306	300	36'10	11	–	2	6,000	21	geared diesel	220	–	3×3in, 8×40mm, 3×21in TT
DE	J. C. *Butler*/WGT	77	1944	1,350	2,100	306	300	36'10	11	–	2	12,000	24	ST	220	–	2×5in, 4×40mm, 3×21in TT

DE	*Rudderow*/TEV	20	1944	1,450	2,230	306	300	36′10	14	–	2	12,000	24	T-E	220	–	2×5in, 4×40mm, 3×21in TT
DE	*Dealey*	13	1954	1,340	1,950	315	308	37	18	–	1	20,000	25	ST	150	–	Weapon A, 4×3in, 6×21in TT
DE	*Claud Jones*	4	1959	1,284	1,755	312	301	38	17′2	–	1	9,200	22	diesel	175	–	2×3in, 6×21in TT
MINE VESSELS																	
CM	*Terror*	1	1942	5,875	8,650	453′10	440	60′2	20	–	2	11,000	20	ST	400	–	4×5in, 24×40mm, 800 mines
DM	*Sumner*	10	1944	2,200	3,370	376′6	369	40′10	19	–	2	60,000	34	ST	350	–	6×5in, 16×40mm, 100 mines
MSF	*Raven-Auk*	64	1940	890	1,250	221′2	215	32′2	11	–	2	3,118	18	D-E	105	–	1×3in, 4×40mm
MSF	*Admirable*	59	1942	650	945	184′6	180	33	10	–	2	1,710	15	diesel	104	–	1×3in, 2×40mm
MSO	*Agile*	62	1953	630	735	172	165	36	10	–	2	1,500	15.5	diesel	72	–	1×40mm
MHC	*Bittern*	1	1957	300	360	144	138	28	8	–	2	1,200	14	diesel	45	–	1×40mm
MSO	*Acme*	4	1956	720	780	173	–	36	14	–	2	2,800	14	diesel	86	–	1×20mm
MSO	*Ability*	3	1957	801	950	190	–	36	12	–	2	2,700	15	diesel	75	–	1×40mm
MSC	*Albatross* (YMS)	58	1942	270	350	136	–	24′6	8	–	2	1,000	15	diesel	50	–	1×3in
MSC	*Bluebird*	22	1953	320	370	144′3	138	28	12	–	2	1,200	14	diesel	40	–	2×20mm
MSC	*Albatross*	2	1960	378	–	145	–	28	13	–	2	1,000	13	diesel	45	–	–
PATROL VESSELS																	
PF	*Tacoma*	27	1943	1,430	2,100	303′11	285′6	37′6	13′6	–	2	5,500	18	recip.	180	–	3×3in, 2×40mm
PC	PC	124	1942	280	450	173′8	170	23	10′9	–	1	2,880	20	diesel	80	–	1×3in, 1×40mm
PC	PCE	29	1943	640	903	184′6	180	33′1	9′5	–	1	2,400	16	diesel	110	–	1×3in, 6×40mm
PC	PCS	19	1943	251	338	136	130	24′6	8′7	–	1	800	14	diesel	60	–	1×3in, 1×40mm
AMPHIBIOUS VESSELS																	
CVHA	*Thetis Bay*	1	1956	8,000	11,000	501	498	65	20	108	2	11,200	18	recip.	1,800+	24	16×40mm
AGC	*Adirondack*	15	1943	5,450	15,295	459	435	63	24′7	–	1	6,000	16	ST	613	–	2×5in, 8×40mm
LSD	*Ashland*	7	1943	4,032	9,375	457′9	454	72′2	18	–	2	7,000	15.4	recip.	240	–	(1×5in), 16×40mm
LSD	*Casa Grande*	13	1944	4,790	8,700	457′9	454	72′2	18	–	2	7,000	15.4	ST	265	–	(1×5in), 12×40mm
LSD	*Thomaston*	8	1954	6,880	11,270	510	–	84	19	–	2	24,000	22.5	ST	404	–	12×3in
LST	LST 1	136	1942	1,625	4,050	328	316	50	14′4	–	2	1,700	10.8	diesel	119	–	7×40mm
LST	LST 1153	2	1947	2,324	6,000	382	368	54	14′5	–	2	6,000	14	ST	190	–	2×5in, 4×40mm
LST	LST 1156	15	1952	2,590	5,800	384	370	55	17	–	2	6,000	14	diesel	116	–	6×3in
LST	LST 1171	7	1957	3,560	7,100	445	–	62	18	–	2	13,700	17	diesel	124	–	6×3in

Type	Class	Number built (converted) or on list 1946	First commissioned	Standard displacement (tons)[1]	Full load displacement (tons)[2]	Overall length (ft)	Waterline length (ft)	Beam (ft)	Maximum draft (ft)	Extreme width (ft)[3]	Propellers	Horsepower[4]	Speed (knots)[5]	Machinery[6]	Complement	Aircraft	Armament[7]
LSM	LSM	161	1944	520	1,095	203′6	196′6	34′6	8′4	–	2	2,800	13	diesel	59	–	2×40mm
LSMR	LSMR	48	1945	994	1,084	211	197′3	34′6	7′2	–	2	2,800	12.6	diesel	138	–	1×5in, 10 rocket-launchers, 4×4.2in mortars, 4×40mm
IFS	*Carronade*	1	1955	1,040	1,500	245	–	38′6	11	–	2	3,100	15	diesel	162	–	1×5in, 8 twin rocket-launchers
APD	APD	92	1944	1,400	2,130	306	300	37	12′7	–	2	12,000	23.6	T-E	214	–	1×5in, 6×40mm
DEPOT SHIPS																	
AD	*Dixie*	5	1940	9,450	17,176	530′6	520	73′3	25′6	–	2	11,000	19.6	ST	1,262	–	4×5in, 10×40mm
AD	*Cascade*	1	1942	9,800	16,650	492	465	70	27	–	1	8,500	16.8	ST	948	–	2×5in, 6×40mm
AD	*Klondike*	10	1945	8,165	16,635	492	465	69′6	27′3	–	1	8,500	18.4	ST	826	–	1×5in, 4×3in, 4×40mm
AR	*Vulcan*	4	1941	9,140	16,200	529′4	520	73′4	23′4	–	2	11,000	19.2	ST	1,297	–	4×5in, 8×40mm
AS	*Fulton*	7	1941	9,734	18,000	530′7	520	73′4	25′6	–	2	11,200	15.4	D-E	1,300	–	4×5in, 10×40mm
ASR	*Chanticleer*	9	1942	1,653	2,140	251′4	240	42	14′10	–	1	3,000	14.9	D-E	102	–	2×3in, 2×40mm
AV	*Curtiss*	2	1940	8,671	13,475	527′4	508	69′3	21′4	–	2	12,000	19.7	ST	1,195	–	4×5in, 14×40mm
AV	*Barnegat*	4	1941	1,766	2,800	310′9	300	41′1	13′6	–	2	6,080	18.2	D-E	215	–	1×5in, 5×40mm
AV	*Currituck*	4	1944	9,106	15,092	540′5	520	69′3	26	–	2	12,000	19.2	ST	1,247	–	4×5in, 20×40mm
AV	*Whiting*	4	1944	8,510	14,000	492	465	69′6	26	–	1	8,500	18.7	ST	1,075	–	2×5in, 12×40mm
SUPPLY SHIPS																	
AE	*Wrangell*	7	1944	6,080	15,277	459′2	435	63	28	–	1	6,000	15	ST	290	–	1×5in, 4×3in, 4×40mm
AE	*Suribachi*	5	1956	7,470	17,400	502	488	72	28	–	1	16,000	21	ST	350	–	4×3in
AKD	*Point Barrow*	1	1958	5,562	14,000	492	475	78	22	–	2	6,000	15	ST	228	–	none
AO	*Cimarron*	24	1941	7,256	25,525	553	525	75	31′6	–	2	13,500	18	ST	274	–	1×5in, 4×3in or 4×5in, 8×40mm
AOG	*Patapsco*	23	1943	1,850	4,335	310′9	292	48′6	15′8	–	2	3,100	14	D-E	124	–	4×3in
AO	*Mispillion*	5	1945	7,243	25,440	553	525	75	32′6	–	2	13,500	16	ST	110	–	1×5in, 4×3in, 8×40mm
AO	*Neosho*	6	1954	11,600	38,000	655	640	86	35	–	2	28,000	20	ST	360	–	4×3in
AO	*Maumee*	4	1956	7,950	32,953	620	591	83′6	32	–	1	20,460	18	ST	52	–	none

MISCELLANEOUS VESSELS

AGB	*Wind*	3	1943	3,500	6,500	269	250	63'6	25'9	–	3	13,300	16	D-E	211	–	2×5in, 12×40mm
AGB	*Glacier*	1	1955	5,100	8,775	310	–	74	29	–	2	21,000	16	D-E	339	–	2×5in, 6×3in
AH	*Sanctuary*	6	1944	11,141	15,400	529	496	71'6	24	–	1	9,000	18.3	ST	530	–	none
AN	*Tree*	25	1941	560	805	163'2	146	30'6	11'8	–	1	800	13	D-E	48	–	1×3in
AN	*Cohoes*	15	1945	650	785	168'6	146	33'10	10'10	–	1	1,200	12	D-E	46	–	1×3in
ARS	*Escape*	20	1943	1,530	1,950	213'6	207	39	14'8	–	2	3,000	15	D-E	120	–	4×40mm
AT	*Apache*	59	1940	1,235	1,675	205	195	38'6	15'4	–	1	3,000	16.5	D-E	85	–	1×3in, 4×40mm
AT	ATA	38	1944	534	835	143	134'6	33'10	13'2	–	1	1,500	13	D-E	45	–	1×3in

US Navy: Basic Data 1963–1988

AIRCRAFT CARRIERS

CV	*Hancock*	7	1943	33,000	42,000	890	820	103	31	185	4	150,000	30+	ST	2,090	~75	4×5in
CV	*Midway*	2	1945	52,500	64,000	979	900	121	35'4	258'6	4	212,000	33	ST	2,645	~75	3×5in
CV	*Midway* (80s)	1	1945	53,400	67,000	1006'8	900	121	36	258'6	4	212,000	32	ST	2,826	~65	2 Sea Sparrow, 2 Phalanx
CV	*Coral Sea* (80s)	1	1947	48,000	65,200	1003'8	900	121	35	236	4	212,000	32	ST	2,502	65	3 Phalanx
CV	*Forrestal*	4	1955	50,000	79,200	1039	990	130	37	238	4	280,000	34	ST	2,760	85	3 Sea Sparrow, 3 Phalanx
CVN	*Enterprise*	1	1961	75,700	90,970	1101'4	1040	133	39	248'4	4	280,000	30+	ST, 2 reactors	3,319	85	2 Sea Sparrow, 3 Phalanx
CV	*Kitty Hawk*	4	1961	60,100	80,800	1045'8	990	130	37	252	4	280,000	30+	ST	2,861	85	3 Sea Sparrow, 3 Phalanx
CVN	*Nimitz*	6	1975	81,800	91,400	1089'3	1040	134	37	250'10	4	280,000	30+	ST, 2 reactors	3,136	85	3 Sea Sparrow, 3 or 4 Phalanx

STRATEGIC MISSILE SUBMARINES

SSBN	*George Washington*	5	1959	6,019	6,688	382	–	33	30	–	1	15,000	20/25+	ST, 1 reactor	139	–	16 Polaris A-3, 6×21in TT
SSBN	*Ethan Allen*	5	1961	6,955	7,900	410'6	–	33	30	–	1	15,000	20/25+	ST, 1 reactor	140	–	16 Polaris A-3, 4×21in TT
SSBN	*Lafayette*	31	1963	7,250	8,250	425	–	33	31'6	–	1	15,000	20/25+	ST, 1 reactor	145	–	16 Poseidon C-3 or Trident C-4, 4×21in TT
SSBN	*Ohio*	20	1981	16,764	18,750	560	–	42	36'4	–	1	–	18/30+	ST, 1 reactor	156	–	24 Trident C-4 or D-5, 4×21in TT

NUCLEAR ATTACK SUBMARINES

SSN	*Nautilus*	1	1954	3,530	4,040	319'5	–	27'6	22	–	2	15,000	18/20+	ST, 1 reactor	120	–	6×21in TT

Type	Class	Number built (converted) or on list 1946	First commissioned	Standard displacement (tons)[1]	Full load displacement (tons)[2]	Overall length (ft)	Waterline length (ft)	Beam (ft)	Maximum draft (ft)	Extreme width (ft)[3]	Propellers	Horsepower[4]	Speed (knots)[5]	Machinery[6]	Complement	Aircraft	Armament[7]
SSN	*Seawolf*	1	1957	3,720	4,280	337′6	–	27′9	22	–	2	15,000	19/20+	ST, 1 reactor	120	–	6×21in TT
SSN	*Skate*	4	1957	2,570	2,860	267′7	–	25	21	–	2	7,500	15.5/20+	ST, 1 reactor	108	–	8×21in TT
SSN	*Skipjack*	6	1959	3,075	3,500	251′9	–	31′6	28	–	1	15,000	15/30+	ST, 1 reactor	112	–	6×21in TT
SSN	*Triton*	1	1959	5,940	6,670	447′6	–	37	24	–	2	34,000	27/20+	ST, 2 reactors	159	–	6×21in TT
SSN	*Halibut*	1	1960	3,850	5,000	350	–	29′6	21′6	–	2	7,500	15.5/15+	ST, 1 reactor	120	–	6×21in TT
SSN	*Tullibee*	1	1960	2,336	2,607	272′9	–	24	20	–	1	2,500	15/20+	T-E, 1 reactor	94	–	4×21in TT
SSN	*Thresher/ Permit*	14	1962	3,750	4,405	278′6	–	31′9	25′2	–	1	15,000	15/30+	ST, 1 reactor	120	–	Harpoon, 4×21in TT, (SUBROC)
SSN	*Sturgeon*	37	1967	4,250	4,780	292′2	–	31′8	29′5	–	1	15,000	15/30+	ST, 1 reactor	130	–	Harpoon, Tomahawk, 4×21in TT, (SUBROC)
SSN	*Narwhal*	1	1969	5,284	5,830	315	–	37′9	26	–	1	17,000	20+/25+	ST, 1 reactor	120	–	Harpoon, Tomahawk, 4×21in TT, (SUBROC)
SSN	G. P. *Lipscomb*	1	1974	5,800	6,480	365	–	31′9	28′10	–	1	12,000	18/25+	T-E, 1 reactor	129	–	Harpoon, Tomahawk, 4×21in TT, (SUBROC)
SSN	*Los Angeles*	66	1976	6,080	6,927	360	–	33	32	–	1	30,000	20/32+	ST, 1 reactor	133	–	Harpoon, Tomahawk, 4×21in TT
SSN	*Seawolf*	~30	1995	–	9,150	326	–	40	35′11	–	1	60,000	–/35	ST, 1 reactor	130	–	Harpoon, Tomahawk, 8×30in TT
DIESEL SUBMARINES																	
SS	*Guppy* IA	2	1951	1,800	2,400	307	–	27	17	–	2	4,610/6,400	20/15	D-E	85	–	10×21in TT
SS	*Guppy* II	10	1951	2,040	2,400	307′6	–	27′4	18	–	2	4,610/6,400	20/15	D-E	85	–	10×21in TT
SS	*Guppy* IIA	10	1951	2,075	2,410	306	–	27	17	–	2	4,800/3,430	18/15	D-E	85	–	10×21in TT
SS	*Guppy* III	9	1951	2,320	2,870	318′10	–	27′3	17	–	2	4,610/6,400	20/15	D-E	84	–	10×21in TT
SS	*Tang*	4	1952	2,100	2,700	287	–	27′2	19	–	2	4,500/5,600	16/16	D-E	87	–	8×21in TT
AGSS	*Albacore*	1	1953	1,500	1,850	210′6	–	27′4	18′6	–	1	1,500/15,000	25/33	D-E	52	–	none

SS	*Sailfish*	2	1956	2,625	3,168	350′6	–	30′0	18	–	2	2,625/3,168	19.5/14	D-E	87	–	6×21in TT
SS	*Barbel*	3	1958	2,145	2,895	219′6	–	29	28	–	2	4,800/3,150	15/25	D-E	85	–	6×21in TT
AGSS	*Dolphin*	1	1968	800	950	152 (165)	–	19′5	18	–	1	/1,650	7.5/15	D-E	24	–	none
BATTLESHIPS																	
BB	*Iowa*	4	1982	48,425	57,350	887′4	860	108′2	38	–	4	212,000	33	ST	1,515	–	Harpoon, Tomahawk, 9×16in, 12×5in, +4 Phalanx
CRUISERS																	
CL	*Cleveland*	7	1942	10,500	13,750	610	600	66	25	–	4	100,000	32	ST	1,200	–	12×6in, 12×5in, 24×40mm
CLAA	*Juneau*	4	1946	6,000	8,000	541	530	53′2	26′8	–	2	75,000	32	ST	700	–	12×5in, 4×3in, 24×40mm
CA	*Baltimore*	10	1943	13,600	17,200	673′5	664	70′10	26′10	–	4	120,000	33	ST	1,146	–	9×8in, 10×5in. 12×3in
CA	*Oregon City*	2	1946	13,700	17,070	673′5	664	70′10	26	–	4	120,000	33	ST	1,925	–	9×8in, 12×5in, 18×3in
CA	*Des Moines*	3	1948	17,000	21,500	716′6	700	75′4	26	–	4	120,000	33	ST	1,300	–	9×8in, 12×5in, 16×3in
GUIDED MISSILE CRUISERS																	
CAG	*Boston*	2	1955	13,300	17,500	673′6	664	70′10	26	–	4	120,000	33	ST	1,273	–	Terrier, 6×8in, 10×5in, 8×3in
CLG	*Galveston*	1	1959	10,500	15,142	610′1	600	66	25	–	4	100,000	32	ST	1,395	–	1 twin Talos, 6×6in, 6×5in
CLG	*Oklahoma City*	2	1959	10,670	14,500	610′1	600	66′4	25	–	4	100,000	32	ST	1,200	–	1 twin Talos, 3×6in, 2×5in
CLG	*Providence*	2	1959	10,670	15,200	610′1	600	66	25′5	–	4	100,000	32	ST	1,145	–	1 twin Terrier, 3×6in, 2×5in
CLG	*Topeka*	1	1960	10,670	14,400	610′1	600	66′6	25	–	4	100,000	32	ST	1,200	–	1 twin Terrier, 6×6in, 6×5in
CGN	*Long Beach*	1	1961	14,200	17,250	721′3	–	73′3	29′8	–	2	80,000	30+	ST, 2 reactors	1,145	–	1 twin Talos, 2 Terrier, ASROC, 2×5in (1984), 2 twin Terrier/ Standard, Harpoon, Tomahawk, 2 Phalanx, 2×5in

Type	Class	Number built (converted) or on list 1946	First commissioned	Standard displacement (tons)[1]	Full load displacement (tons)[2]	Overall length (ft)	Waterline length (ft)	Beam (ft)	Maximum draft (ft)	Extreme width (ft)[3]	Propellers	Horsepower[4]	Speed (knots)[5]	Machinery[6]	Complement	Aircraft	Armament[7]
CG	*Albany*	3	1962	13,700	18,950	674	663	71	27	–	4	120,000	30.4	ST	1,250	–	2 twin Talos, 2 twin Tartar, ASROC, 2×5in, 6 TT
CG	*Leahy*	9	1962	5,670	7,800	533	–	55	24′6	–	2	85,000	32	ST	415	–	2 twin Terrier/ Standard, ASROC, 4×3in, 6 TT (1967) 2 twin Terrier/ Standard, ASROC + Harpoon, +2 Phalanx
CGN	*Bainbridge*	1	1962	7,700	8,580	565	550	58	29	–	2	60,000	30+	ST, 2 reactors	480	–	2 twin Terrier/ Standard, ASROC, 2×5in, 6 TT (1983), 2 twin Terrier/ Standard, ASROC (4×3in), + Harpoon, +2 Phalanx
CG	*Belknap*	9	1964	6,570	7,930	547	–	54′9	28′9	–	2	85,000	33	ST	418	–	1 twin Terrier/ Standard, ASROC, 1×5in, 6×TT, +Harpoon, +2 Phalanx
CGN	*Truxtun*	1	1967	8,200	9,200	564	–	58	31	–	2	60,000	30+	ST, 2 reactors	510	–	1 twin Terrier/ Standard, ASROC, 1×5in, 4 TT, +Harpoon, +2 Phalanx

CGN	*California*	2	1974	8,700	10,530	596	–	61	31'6	–	2	60,000	30+	ST, 2 reactors	595	–	2 Tartar/Standard, ASROC, 2×5in, 4 TT, +Harpoon, +2 Phalanx
CGN	*Virginia*	4	1976	8,620	11,300	585	–	63	29'6	–	2	60,000	30+	ST, 2 reactors	565	–	2 Tartar/Standard, ASROC, 2×5in, 4 TT, +Harpoon, +2 Phalanx
CG	*Ticonderoga*	27	1983	–	9,500	565'10	532'8	55	31'6	–	2	80,000	30+	gas turbine	364	–	2 twin Standard/ MR or 2 61-cell VLS, 2×5in, Harpoon, 2 Phalanx
COMMAND SHIPS																	
CC	*Northampton*	1	1953	14,700	17,200	676	664	71	29	–	4	120,000	31.6	ST	1,191	–	1×5in
CC	*Wright*	1	1963	14,500	19,750	683'6	664	78'9	28	–	4	120,000	30.8	ST	1,720	–	8×40mm
LCC	*Blue Ridge*	2	1970	–	19,290	620	–	82	27	–	1	22,000	20	ST	720	–	2 Sea Sparrow, 4×3in, +2 Phalanx
DESTROYERS																	
DD	*Fletcher*703	88	1942	2,050	3,040	376'6	369	39'4	18	–	2	60,000	35	ST	300	–	5×5in, 10×40mm, 5 TT
DD	*Sumner* (FRAM)	53	1944	2,300	3,300	376'6	369	41'4	21	–	2	60,000	32.5	ST	305	–	6×5in, Hedgehog
DD	*Gearing* (FRAM)	95	1944	2,425	3,410+	390'6	383	40'10	19	–	2	60,000	34	ST	307	–	4×5in, ASROC, 6 TT
DD	*Forrest Sherman*	14	1955	2,800	4,050	418	407	45'2	22	–	2	70,000	32.5	ST	292	–	3×5in, 2×3in, ASROC, 6 TT
DD	*Spruance*	31	1975	5,770	8,040	563'4	529	55	29	–	2	80,000	32.5	GT	334	–	Harpoon, Sea Sparrow, +2 Phalanx, 2×5in, 6 TT or VLS
DD	*Arleigh Burke*	29	1990	–	8,300	466	–	59	30'7	–	2	100,000	30+	GT	325	–	VLS, Standard/ Tomahawk, Harpoon, 1×5in, 2 Phalanx, 6 TT

Type	Class	Number built (converted) or on list 1946	First commissioned	Standard displacement (tons)[1]	Full load displacement (tons)[2]	Overall length (ft)	Waterline length (ft)	Beam (ft)	Maximum draft (ft)	Extreme width (ft)[3]	Propellers	Horsepower[4]	Speed (knots)[5]	Machinery[6]	Complement	Aircraft	Armament[7]
GUIDED-MISSILE DESTROYERS																	
DDG	*C. F. Adams*	23	1960	3,370	4,500	437	420	47	20	–	2	70,000	31.5	ST	354	–	1 twin Tartar/ Standard, 2×5in, ASROC, 6 TT
DDG	*Coontz*	10	1960	4,700	5,800	512′6	–	52′6	25	–	2	85,000	33	ST	398	–	1 twin Terrier/ Standard, 1×5in, ASROC, 6 TT, +Harpoon
DDG	*Decatur* exDD	4	1967	2,850	4,150	418	407	45	20	–	2	70,000	32.5	ST	335	–	1 Tartar/Standard, 1×5in, ASROC, 6 TT
DDG	*Mitscher* exDD	2	1968	–	5,200	493	476	50	21	–	2	80,000	33	ST	377	–	1 Terrier/ Standard, ASROC, 2×5in
DDG	*Kidd*	4	1981	–	9,574	563′4	529	55	30	–	2	80,000	30+	GT	339	–	2 Standard/ Tomahawk, Harpoon, 2×5in, 2 Phalanx, 6 TT, ASROC
ESCORTS/FRIGATES																	
DE	*Buckley*	57	1942	1,400	2,170	306	300	36′10	14	–	2	12,000	23.5	ST	213	–	3×3in, 6×40mm
DE	*J. C. Butler*	77	1944	1,350	2,100	306	300	36′10	14	–	2	12,000	24	ST	220	–	2×5in
DE	*Rudderow*	19	1944	1,450	1,990	306	300	36′10	14	–	2	12,000	24	ST	216	–	2×5in, 4×40mm
DE	*Dealey*	13	1954	1,340	1,940	314′6	308	37	18′10	–	1	20,000	26	ST	172	–	Weapon A, 2×3in
DE	*Claud Jones*	4	1959	1,284	1,755	312	301	38	18	–	1	9,200	22	diesel	175	–	2×3in
FF	*Bronstein*	2	1963	2,360	2,650	371′6	350	40′6	23	–	1	20,000	24	ST	199	–	ASROC, 2×3in, 6 TT
FF	*Garcia*	10	1964	2,620	3,400	414′6	394	44′2	24	–	1	35,000	27	ST	247	–	ASROC, 2×5in, 6 TT
AGFF	*Glover*	1	1965	2,643	3,426	414′6	400	44′2	14	–	1	35,000	27	ST	236	–	ASROC, 1×5in, 6 TT
FF	*Knox*	46	1969	3,011	4,100	438	415	46′9	24′9	–	1	35,000	27	ST	217	–	1 Sea Sparrow, ASROC/ Harpoon, 1×5in,

FFG	*Brooke*	6	1966	2,640	3,245	414'6	390	44'2	24	–	1	35,000	27	ST	236	–	1 Tartar/Standard, ASROC, 1×5in
FFG	*Perry*	58	1977	2,647	3,605	453	413	45	24'6	–	1	40,000	28	GT	176	–	1 Standard/MR, 1 Phalanx, 1×76mm
AMPHIBIOUS VESSELS																	
LPH	*Iwo Jima*	7	1961	17,000	18,300	592	556	83'8	26	104	1	22,000	20	ST	528	25	2 Sea Sparrow, +2 Phalanx, 4×3in
LHA	*Tarawa*	5	1976	25,120	39,400	833'9	777'2	106	26	132	2	70,000	24	ST	940	35	2 Sea Sparrow, 1 Phalanx, 3×5in
LHD	*Wasp*	5	1989	25,800	40,530	844	777'2	106	26'8	140	2	71,000	22+	ST	1081	40	2 Sea Sparrow, 3 Phalanx
LPD	*Raleigh*	3	1962	8,275	14,650	521'9	500	84	21'7	–	2	24,000	20	ST	490	–	6×3in, +2 Phalanx
LPD	*Austin*	11	1965	10,000	16,900	568'9	–	84	23	–	2	24,000	20	ST	490	–	4×3in, +2 Phalanx
LPR	*APD*	64	1944	1,400	2,130	306	300	37	13	–	2	12,000	23.6	ST	121	–	1×5in, 6×40mm
LSD	*Ashland*	8	1943	4,032	9,375	457'9	454	72'2	18	–	2	7,000	15.4	recip	240	–	12×40mm
LSD	*Casa Grande*	13	1944	4,790	8,700	457'9	454	72'2	18	–	2	7,000	15.4	ST	265	–	12×40mm
LSD	*Thomaston*	8	1954	6,880	11,270	510	–	84	19	–	2	24,000	22.5	ST	404	–	6×3in
LSD	*Anchorage*	5	1968	8,600	14,000	553'4	534	85	18'6	–	2	24,000	22	ST	358	–	6×3in, +2 Phalanx
LSD	*Whidbey Island*	8	1985	11,275	15,704	609'7	580	84	20	–	2	33,600	20+	diesel	342	–	2 Phalanx
LSMR	*Elk River*	12	1945	994	1,280	211	197'3	34'5	8'8	–	2	2,880	13.9	diesel	138	–	1×5in, 4×40mm, 10 rocket-launchers
LST	*LST 1*	53	1942	1,653	2,080	328	316	50	14'4	–	2	1,700	11.6	diesel	115	–	8×40mm
LST	*Talbot County*	2	1947	2,250	6,000	382	368	54	17'3	–	2	6,000	14.3	ST	184	–	2×5in, 8×40mm
LST	*Terrebonne Parish*	15	1953	2,580	5,800	384	370	55	17	–	2	6,000	15	diesel	157	–	6×3in
LST	*Suffolk County*	7	1957	4,164	8,000	445	–	62	16'6	–	2	14,440	17.5	diesel	184	–	6×3in
LST	*Newport*	20	1969	4,793	8,342	522'4	–	69'6	17'6	–	2	16,500	20	diesel	223	–	4×3in, +1 Phalanx
MINE VESSELS																	
MCS	*Catskill*	2	1966	5,875	9,040	455'5	440	60'2	20	–	2	11,000	19.6	ST	586	–	2×5in, 8×40mm
MSF	*Raven-Auk*	59	1940	890	1,250	221'2	215	32'2	11	–	2	3,200	18.0	D-E	105	–	1×3in
MSF	*Admirable*	57	1942	650	945	184'6	180	33	10	–	2	1,710	15.0	diesel	104	–	1×3in
MSO	*Agile*	62	1953	665	750	172	165	35	14	–	2	2,280	15.5	diesel	78	–	1×40mm
MSO	*Acme*	4	1957	720	780	173	–	36	14	–	2	2,800	14	diesel	86	–	1×20mm
MSO	*Ability*	3	1958	801	950	190	–	36	12	–	2	2,700	15	diesel	75	–	1×40mm
MCM	*Avenger*	14	1987	–	1,312	224'4	212'9	39	11'6	–	2	2,600	13.5	diesel	72	–	none

Type	Class	Number built (converted) or on list 1946	First commissioned	Standard displacement (tons)[1]	Full load displacement (tons)[2]	Overall length (ft)	Waterline length (ft)	Beam (ft)	Maximum draft (ft)	Extreme width (ft)[3]	Propellers	Horsepower[4]	Speed (knots)[5]	Machinery[6]	Complement	Aircraft	Armament[7]
PATROL VESSELS																	
PG	*Asheville*	2	1969	225	245	164′2	148	23′11	9′2	–	2	1,750/14,000	16/40+	diesel/GT	29	–	1×3in, 1×40mm
PTF	*Nasty*	13	1963	–	85	80′4	–	24′6	6′9	–	2	6,200	45	diesel	19	–	1×40mm, 2×20mm, 1×81mm mortar
PTF	*Osprey*	4	1968	80	105	94′9	–	23′2	7	–	2	6,200	40	diesel	19	–	1×40mm, 2×20mm, 1×81mm
PCH	*High Point*	1	1963	–	100	115	–	31	6	–	–	600/6,200	12/48	diesel/GT	13	–	MG
PGH	*Flagstaff*	2	1968	–	57	74′4	–	22	4′2	–	1	300/3,620	8/52	diesel/GT	13	–	1×40mm
AGEH	*Plainview*	1	1969	–	320	212	–	40	25	–	–	1,200/30,000	12/50+	diesel/GT	20	–	none
PHM	*Pegasus*	6	1977	198	265	147′2	118	28′2	23′2	–	–	1,600/16,767	12/40+	diesel/GT	23	–	8 Harpoon, 1×76mm
DEPOT SHIPS																	
AD	*Dixie*	5	1940	9,450	17,176	530′6	520	73′4	25′6	–	2	11,000	19.6	ST	1,070	–	4×20mm
AD	*Klondike*	2	1945	8,165	16,635	492	465	69′6	27′2	–	1	8,500	18.4	ST	918	–	1×5in, 2×3in
AD	*Gompers*	6	1967	13,600	22,260	643	–	85	22′6	–	1	20,000	20	ST	1,367	–	(1×5in), 2×40mm
AR	*Vulcan*	4	1941	9,140	16,200	529′6	520	73′4	23′4	–	2	11,000	19.2	ST	715	–	(4×5in), 4×20mm
AS	*Fulton*	6	1941	9,734	18,000	529′6	–	73′4	25′6	–	2	11,200	15	D-E	917	–	(2×5in), 4×20mm
AS	*Proteus*	1	1960	10,234	18,500	574′6	–	73′4	25′6	–	2	11,200	15	D-E	1,121	–	(2×5in), 4×20mm
AS	*Hunley*	2	1962	10,500	18,300	599	–	83	24	–	1	15,000	19	D-E	1,081	–	4×20mm
AS	*Simon Lake*	2	1964	12,000	21,500	643′9	–	85	30	–	1	20,000	18	ST	1,075	–	4×3in
AS	*L. Y. Spear*	5	1970	12,770	22,628	645′8	–	85	25	–	1	20,000	18	ST	1,072	–	4×20mm
ASR	*Chanticleer*	4	1943	1,635	2,290	251′4	–	42	14′11	–	1	3,000	15	D-E	85	–	2×20mm
ASR	*Pigeon*	2	1973	3,411	4,570	251	–	86′4	21′3	–	2	6,000	15	diesel	195	–	2×20mm
SUPPLY VESSELS																	
AO	*Cimarron*	24	1941	7,256	25,525	553	549	75	31′6	–	2	13,500	18	ST	274	–	4×3in
AO	*Mispillion*	5	1945	11,000	35,090	646	–	75	35′6	–	2	13,500	16	ST	111	–	(4×3in)
AO	*Neosho*	6	1954	11,600	38,000	655	–	86	35	–	2	28,000	20	ST	360	–	(4×3in)

AO	*Cimarron* (new)	5	1981	8,210	27,500	591′4	549	88	33′6	–	1	24,000	20	ST	212	–	2 Phalanx
AO	*Kaiser*	19	1986	9,500	40,700	677′6	–	97′6	35	–	2	32,000	20	diesel	119	–	none
AOE	*Sacramento*	5	1964	19,200	53,600	793′9	705	107	39′4	–	2	100,000	26	ST	600	–	(8×3in), 1 Sea Sparrow, +2 Phalanx
AOR	*Wichita*	7	1969	12,500	41,350	659	–	96	33′4	–	2	32,000	20	ST	345	–	(4×3in), 2 Phalanx
AKR	*Algol*	8	1984	31,000	55,000	946′2	–	105′2	36′8	–	2	120,000	33	ST	45	–	none
PPS	*Hauge*	5	1984	28,249	46,484	755′6	–	90′1	32′1	–	1	16,800	17.5	diesel	49	–	none
PPS	*Kocak*	3	1984	15,000	48,754	821	–	105′6	32′2	–	1	30,000	20	ST	59	–	none
PPS	*Bobo*	5	1985	22,700	40,846	673	–	105′6	29′6	–	1	26,040	18.8	diesel	55	–	none
AE	*Suribachi*	5	1956	10,000	17,500	512	–	72	29	–	1	16,000	20.6	ST	316	–	4×3in
AE	*Kilauea*	8	1968	9,338	19,937	564	–	81	25′9	–	1	22,000	20	ST	401	–	4×3in, +2 Phalanx
AFS	*Mars*	7	1963	9,200	16,070	581	–	79	24	–	1	22,000	20	ST	430	–	4×3in, +2 Phalanx
AFS	*Sirius*	3	1981	9,010	16,792	524	–	72	22	–	1	11,520	19	diesel	169	–	none
MISCELLANEOUS VESSELS																	
AT	*Navajo*	15	1940	1,235	1,675	205	195	38′6	15′2	–	1	3,000	15	D-E	67	–	1×3in
AT	ATA	4	1944	534	835	143	134′6	33′10	14	–	1	1,500	13	D-E	45	–	1×3in or 4×20mm
ATF	*Powhatan*	7	1979	2,000	2,260	240′6	225	42	15	–	2	4,500	15	diesel	21	–	none
ATS	*Edenton*	3	1971	2,650	3,117	282′8	264	50	15′2	–	2	6,000	16	diesel	115		2 or 4×20mm
ARS	*Escape*	7	1944	1,530	2,045	213′6	207	43	13	–	2	3,000	16	D-E	69	–	2×20mm
ARS	*Safeguard*	4	1985	2,300	2,880	254′11	239′6	51	15′5	–	2	4,200	13.5	geared diesel	90	–	none
AGB	*Wind*	6	1943	3,500	6,500	269	250	63′6	25′9	–	2	10,000	16	D-E	–	–	
AGB	*Glacier*	1	1955	5,100	8,775	310	288	74	29′0	–	2	21,000	16	D-E	339	–	2×5in, 6×3in
AGOS	*Stalwart*	19	1984	1,600	2,285	224	203	43	15	–	2	3,200	11	D-E	26	–	none
AGS	*Maury*	2	1989	8,810	15,821	449′9	–	72	30′6	–	1	25,000	21	diesel	108	–	none
AH	*Mercy*	2	1988	24,712	69,320	894	–	105′9	32′10	–	1	24,500	17.5	ST	1159	–	none

Notes 1946–1962
[1] Submarines: displacement surfaced. [2] Submarines: displacement submerged. [3] Aircraft carriers. [4] Submarines: surfaced/submerged. [5] Submarines: surfaced/submerged. [6] ST, steam turbines; D-E, diesel-electric; T-E, turbo-electric; GT, gas turbines; recip, reciprocating. [7] ( ), removed later; +, added later.

Notes 1963–1988
[1] Submarines: displacement surfaced. [2] Submarines: displacement submerged. [3] Aircraft carriers. [4] Submarines: surfaced/submerged. [5] Submarines: surfaced/submerged; hydrofoils: foilborne. [6] ST, steam turbines; DE, diesel-electric; T-E, turbo-electric; GT, gas turbines; recip, reciprocating. [7] ( ), removed later; +, added later.

92. *Charles F. Adams* (DDG 2), nameship of the largest class of missile ships to that time. Built between 1958 and 1964, twenty-three destroyers of the class entered service. They were armed with one twin launcher for Tartar SAM aft, two single 5in guns and one ASROC launcher amidships as well as two triple torpedo tube mounts. Six additional ships of this class were built, three each for Australia and West Germany.

93. New York City firemen fighting a fire on 19 December 1960, on board the aircraft carrier *Constellation* (CVA 64) which was fitting out at Brooklyn, New York. Notice the lowered deck elevator, looking aft. She was the second of four carriers of the *Kitty Hawk* class, somewhat larger than the earlier *Forrestals* with a different arrangement of deck elevators. Her aircraft flew the first strikes against North Vietnam in August 1964.

94. A single prototype nuclear submarine designed to operate off enemy ports or in confined waterways was the *Tullibee* (SSN 597), completed in 1960. She was considerably smaller than other nuclear submarines and was the first fitted with turbo-electric machinery. The design was not repeated and the ship was decommissioned in 1987.

95. The refitted aircraft carrier *Coral Sea* (CVA 43) launching aircraft. Notice her streamlined appearance and enclosed bow. All guns have been removed from along the side of the ship.

96. With the growing Soviet submarine fleet looming as a major threat, anti-submarine warfare occupied a major focus of the navy's activities. Older *Essex*-class carriers were converted for ASW use. Here a task group led by *Valley Forge* (CVS 45) conducts training exercises in 1959 in the Atlantic with a squadron of *Fletcher*-class escort destroyers. They are (l. to r.) *Murray* (DDE 576), *Beale* (471), *Eaton* (510), *Conway* (507), *Cony* (508) and *Waller* (466), all armed with Weapon A in place of number two gun mount.

94

95

96

1958–63

97. The seaplane tender *Duxbury Bay* (AVP 38) painted white while serving as flagship in the Middle East. Together with *Greenwich Bay* and *Valcour*, duties of flagship were rotated.

1960

98. Destroyer tender *Shenandoah* (AD 26) shares a pier with the destroyers *Richard E. Kraus* (DD 849) and *Steinaker* (DD 863). She was one of ten tenders built during the war on modified C-3 merchant hulls.

99. The newly lengthened submarine tender *Proteus* (AS 19) following her conversion in 1960 to service ballistic-missile submarines. A 44-foot section was added amidships to provide added working space as well as storage space for Polaris missiles. A travelling crane was installed to transport the missiles. The 5in gun forward was removed in the 1970s.

1961

100. A landmark was passed in September 1961 with the commissioning of the guided-missile cruiser *Long Beach*

(CLGN 9), the navy's first nuclear-powered surface vessel. She was also the first warship to be armed solely with guided missiles. Originally to be armed with Regulus II SSM, she was completed with two twin Terrier launchers forward and a twin Talos launcher aft. An ASROC launcher is mounted amidships. The squared panels on the superstructure are radar antennae. Two 5in guns were subsequently mounted amidships. (USN 1056114)

101. A second landmark was achieved on 25 November 1961 with the commissioning of the world's largest warship and the first nuclear-powered aircraft carrier, *Enterprise* (CVAN 65). Her four steam turbines are powered by eight water-cooled reactors. It was originally proposed to build six of these carriers, but at a cost of $451 million each this was deferred. She was the first carrier to deploy the F-14 Tomcat whose wings change configuration as needed to provide optimum wing form. Here she takes on supplies from the ammunition ship *Shasta* (AE 6) early in 1962. Notice that three of the four deck-edge elevators are lowered.

102. A Terrier missile is launched from the bows of the nuclear cruiser *Long Beach*. Introduced in 1955, this missile was the only ship-based surface-to-air nuclear missile still operational in the late 1980s, and is being replaced by the non-nuclear Standard-ER missile.

103. Tender *Bryce Canyon* (AD 36), with Destroyer Division 2 alongside, at Long Beach, California, in 1961 following FRAM refits. *Lyman K. Swenson* (DD 729), *Collett* (DD 730) and *Blue* (DD 744) of the *Sumner class* and the larger *Gearing*-class *Shelton* (DD 790) show off their topsides. The latter has only two gun mounts and ASROC amidships. Notice VDS gear on fantail of *Blue*. A five-gun *Fletcher*-class vessel, *Colahan* (DD 658), is at top of picture.

104. During the early 1960s the Fleet Rehabilitation and Modernization programme (FRAM) was carried out to prolong the service life of Second World War-built ships. *Gearing*-class destroyers were the chief beneficiaries of this programme and all but two special types were modernized. *Bordelon* (DD 881) is typical of the majority of the conversions (FRAM I), retaining two 5in mounts, one forward and one aft. ASROC launcher has been added between the stacks and DASH hangar and and platform aft. New, short torpedo tubes are forward of the bridge.

105. *Bausell* (DD 845) was one of eight to keep all four guns forward, but other modifications were similar. The torpedo tubes are positioned next to the second funnel.

106. *Douglas H. Fox* (DD 779) typifies the FRAM II conversion given to 33 short-hull *Sumner*-class destroyers. They retained all six 5in guns with helicopter hangar added aft and VDS gear on the stern.

102

103

104

105

106

107. The *Iwo Jima* class of amphibious assault ships, built between 1959 and 1970, introduced a new type of ship, the first ships designed as helicopter carriers. Each vessel can carry 11 to 19 helicopters and a Marine battalion but no landing craft. *Guam* (LPH 9) is one of seven which formed the nucleus of the navy's amphibious forces. Notice port-side deck-edge elevator, and 3in guns forward of island.

1962

108. The frigate *Bainbridge* (DLGN 25) as completed was a repetition of the *Leahy* class with nuclear propulsion. As with the other frigates she was reclassified a cruiser in 1975. In 1974–6 she was extensively modernized with a new superstructure amidships and pole mainmast.

107

109

110

109. *Chicago* (CG 11) was one of three heavy cruisers stripped down to the main deck and rebuilt as missile cruisers in 1962–4. The new superstructure was aluminium and the two tall 'Macks' rose 104 feet from main deck level. Armed with two twin Talos and two twin Tartar SAM launchers, they subsequently had two 5in guns added, seen at base of the second Mack. A Tartar launcher is next to the massive superstructure.

110. An impressive demonstration as the guided-missile cruiser *Albany* (CG 10) fires three Terrier and Tartar missiles simultaneously.

111

112

113

114

115

111. The seaplane tender *Norton Sound* (AVM 1) was converted to a missile testing ship in 1951. In 1962–4 she was fitted with a SPG-59 Typhon guidance system (above). During 1974 she was again modified to test the Aegis air-defence system. More recently she tested vertical launch systems for cruisers and destroyers and was finally decommissioned in 1986.

112. *Gridley* (DLG 21), one of nine frigates of the *Leahy* class, built in 1959–64, which introduced the 'Mack' structure combining mast and exhaust funnel. They were reclassified cruisers (CG) in 1975, becoming the navy's smallest cruisers. Originally armed with two twin launchers for Terrier/Standard missiles and one ASROC launcher, the two twin 3in mounts were removed in 1977–8. Notice the missile reloading mechanism between the two launchers forward.

1963

113. One by one the Second World War ships were taken away to the scrapyard, but some never reached their destination. Here in January 1963 the old escort carrier *Makassar Strait* (CVE 91) is ashore and broken in two on San Nicholas Island, California, after serving as a target ship. (USN 1081677)

114. On 10 April 1963 the Navy suffered a significant disaster with the loss with all hands of the nuclear submarine *Thresher* (SSN 593), lead ship of a new class. Hardly a year old, she was the first nuclear submarine to be lost. The new design included torpedo tubes amidships and bow-mounted sonar. Following her loss completion of units under construction was held up pending design improvements and the class name was changed to *Permit* class.

1964

115. *Sacramento* (AOE 1), completed in 1964, is the world's largest replenishment ship. On a length of 794 feet, she displaces 53,600 tons full load. Her machinery was built for the cancelled battleship *Kentucky*. Three additional ships of the class were built between 1962 and 1970. These enormous vessels can carry 194,000 barrels of fuel oil, 2,100 tons of munitions plus other stores. They have a speed of 27.5 knots. Notice the Sea Sparrow SAM launcher forward, fitted in 1979.

116. The newly completed *Lafayette*-class strategic missile submarine *Will Rogers* (SSBN 659) puts to sea in 1967. Originally built to carry the Polaris A-2 or A-3 missile, this class was modified to Poseidon C-3 during 1970–8. Commissioned between 1963 and 1967, the 31 ships of the class have operated without incident for more than twenty years. They were designed for a 20-year service life, later extended to 30 years. Four additional vessels were cancelled in 1965. The last twelve submarines of the class have quieter machinery and are being upgraded to carry Trident C-4 missiles. *Nathan Hale* (SSBN 623) was decommissioned in 1986 and others will go out of service as *Ohio*-class vessels are completed.

117. The Gulf of Tonkin incident on 2 August 1964 involved an attack upon the destroyer *Maddox* (DD-731) by three North Vietnamese gunboats in international waters thirty miles off the coast. This picture was taken from *Maddox* during the attack. The following day *Maddox* and *Turner Joy* (DD 951) were again attacked by six torpedo-boats while sixty miles off the coast. Aircraft from the carrier *Ticonderoga* attacked support facilities for patrol boats the same day. (USN 711524)

118. The large and continuing programme for developing and testing missiles of various types and sizes and the space programme required conversion of ships for tracking and observing missiles and satellites. They are civilian manned and operated by the MSTS. *Wheeling* (AGM 8) was a converted Victory Ship used for recording data from missiles and satellites out of range of land stations.

119. The strategic missile submarine *Henry Clay* (SSBN 625) successfully launches a Polaris A-3 missile while on the surface. There is a temporary telemetry antenna on the sail and the missile tube hatch is open.

1965

120. New types of ships were added to the amphibious forces such as the amphibious transport dock. *Denver* (LPD 9) was one of eleven ships of the *Austin* class built similar to the older dock landing ships. They were considerably larger, with a fixed flight deck above the docking well, and could carry 800–900 troops.

121. Looking forward in the docking well of the amphibious transport dock *Shreveport* (LPD 12) in 1972, with four LCU embarked. Notice the vehicles and men relaxing forward. (USN 1152178)

116

117

118

119

120

121

122

123

122. During a 1960s refit the pole foremast in the cruiser *Saint Paul* (CA 73) was replaced by a heavy pylon structure to support increased radar equipment. Notice campaign ribbons on the bridge.

123. The submarine tender *Simon Lake* (AS 33) with her brood at Holy Loch, Scotland. Four diesel units are at right, the others are nuclear types. At left is the submarine rescue vessel *Tringa* (ASR 16). Bases for nuclear submarines were also set up in Spain, Italy and Japan.

124. The large 'frigates', later cruisers, of the *Belknap* class were designed as escorts for aircraft carriers with anti-aircraft and anti-submarine capabilities. Nine ships of 7,930 tons full load were built, armed with a twin Terrier/Asroc launcher forward and a single 5in gun aft. Two Harpoon canisters were mounted amidships in 1982, replacing the original 3in guns, and two Phalanx CIWS were added in 1984 Here is *Belknap* (DLG 26) with Terrier missiles in place, arriving at Hong Kong.

125. Sixteen frigates (originally described as escorts) of the *Garcia* and *Brooke* classes were built during the 1960s. They differed mainly in armament, the six *Brooke*-class vessels having a Tartar/Standard launcher aft in place of the second 5in gun in the *Garcia* class. The ASROC launcher is mounted forward and the original DASH hangar aft was enlarged to accommodate the larger SH-2F helicopter. This is *Garica* (DE 1040) as completed in 1964. Ten more missile-armed units were planned in 1964, but they were not built for reasons of cost. These ships were decommissioned in 1988 and lent to foreign countries.

124

125

126

127

128

1966

126. After the war large numbers of obsolete and new ships were laid up and put in 'mothballs'. In 1966 there still remained a large reserve fleet part of which is seen here at the Philadelphia Naval Shipyard. The battleships *Iowa*, *New Jersey* and *Wisconsin* can be seen at lower left while in the inner basin are rows of cruisers, destroyers and destroyer escorts. Two light carriers are at far left. At the piers at bottom are several aircraft carriers and some smaller ships. (CSF-4037-7-66)

127. With the appearance of a hostile regime in Cuba less than 150 miles from the coast of the United States, a small combatant vessel for coastal patrol and blockade missions was needed. To meet this the *Asheville*-class gunboats were built in 1965–70. With aluminium hulls and aluminium-fibreglass superstructures and a combination of diesel and gas-turbine machinery, they were very fast and were able to accelerate from standing still to 40 knots in one minute. These gunboats were used in Vietnam and in the Mediterranean, such as *Surprise* (PG 97), seen here on trials in 1969. *Antelope*, *Ready*, *Grand Rapids* and *Douglas* of this class were armed with two Standard/ARM launchers in 1972.

128. As part of the NECPA programme, the light carrier *Saipan* (CVL 48) was converted to provide communications relay equipment for commands afloat. Recommissioned as *Arlington* (AGMR 2) in August 1966, she remained in commission less than four years. The open flight deck provided unobstructed space for the various antennae.

129. The guided-missile escort (later frigate) *Brooke* (DEG 1) fires an ASROC missile during a demonstration in June 1969. This anti-submarine rocket was fitted in all cruisers and destroyers during the 1960s. A short-range weapon with a range of six miles, it is fired from an eight-tube box launcher, although later ships use missile-launchers. It can fire either a nuclear or high-explosive warhead, but the nuclear warhead was to be discontinued in 1989.

1967

130. A new series of tenders was built starting in the 1960s. *Samuel Gompers* (AD 37), completed in 1967, was first of a new class of six destroyer tenders. Considerably larger than previous tenders, they have their steam turbine engines aft. Notice the massive cranes amidships and single 5in gun forward.

131. The navy's fourth nuclear-powered warship, *Truxtun* (DLGN 35), was similar to the *Belknap* class with the armament in reversed positions. Planned by the navy with conventional machinery, nuclear propulsion was directed by Congress. The two lattice masts give the ship a unique appearance as she leaves her builder's yard at Camden, New Jersey in 1967. ASROC missiles can be fired from the Terrier launcher aft. Harpoon canisters replaced the 3in guns amidships in 1975 and Phalanx CIWS was added in 1989. (USN 1122319)

132. *Somers* (DDG 34) was one of four *Forrest Sherman*-class destroyers converted to missile destroyers in 1967. A Tartar launcher, helicopter hangar and ASROC launcher replaced two 5in guns aft and two tall trellis masts were added. Conversion of others was cancelled because of the high cost and limitations of the Tartar system.

133. On 8 June 1967 the electronic intelligence ship *Liberty* (AGTR 5) was attacked by Israeli aircraft and torpedo-boats off the coast of Sinai resulting in the deaths of 34 crew members. It was the worst peacetime incident of the century involving the navy. Israel said it was a clear case of mistaken identity and apologized for the attack. Here the *Liberty* lies dead in the water, as a helicopter hovers nearby.

131

135

134. *Forrestal* (CVA 59), first of the supercarriers, was severely damaged by fire on 29 July 1967 while operating in the Gulf of Tonkin. 134 sailors died in the disaster. Here the destroyer *Rupertus* (DD 851) stands by to assist fighting the fires. The accident occurred when a Zuni rocket, inadvertently fired from an aircraft being readied for takeoff, struck the fully loaded tank of another aircraft which exploded. (USN 1124777)

135. During the 1960s minesweeper tenders, designated mine countermeasures and support ships, were brought into service. *Ozark* (MCS 2) was one of the two old landing ship vehicles reinstated on the list and rebuilt. Designed to serve as a mobile support base for minesweepers, she carried 20 MSLs and 2 helicopters. Two landing ships, *Orleans Parish* (LST 1069) and *Epping Forest* (LSD 4), were converted pending conversion of the larger ships. They had all been decommissioned by 1970 with the phaseout of the minesweeper programmes.

136. Submarine development continued and in 1967 the first of 37 units of the *Sturgeon* class was delivered. *Flying Fish* (SSN 673) is a typical unit of this improved *Permit* class, which can be distinguished by the taller sail. The diving planes mounted on the sail can be turned into the vertical position for breaking through polar ice. They carry Harpoon and Tomahawk missiles which are launched through the torpedo tubes.

137. The Coast Guard cutter *Point Kennedy* (WPB 82320) alongside the rocket support ship *St. Francis River* (LFR 525) in the Mekong Delta in January 1967. *Point Kennedy* was one of 26 82-footers shipped out to Vietnam in 1965. All were transferred to the Vietnamese Navy in 1969–71.

138. The heavy cruiser *Saint Paul* (CA 73) coming under fire from coastal defence batteries while shelling the Cong Phu railroad yard on 4 August 1967. She received superficial damage but her accompanying destroyers, USS *Blue* and HMAS *Hobart* were not hit.

139. The minesweeping boat MSB-21 engaged in sweeping the Long Tau River below Saigon for Vietcong mines in November 1967. These boats were originally designed to be carried on larger ships but were too big for handling with cranes. At least four were lost in Vietnam.

137

138

139

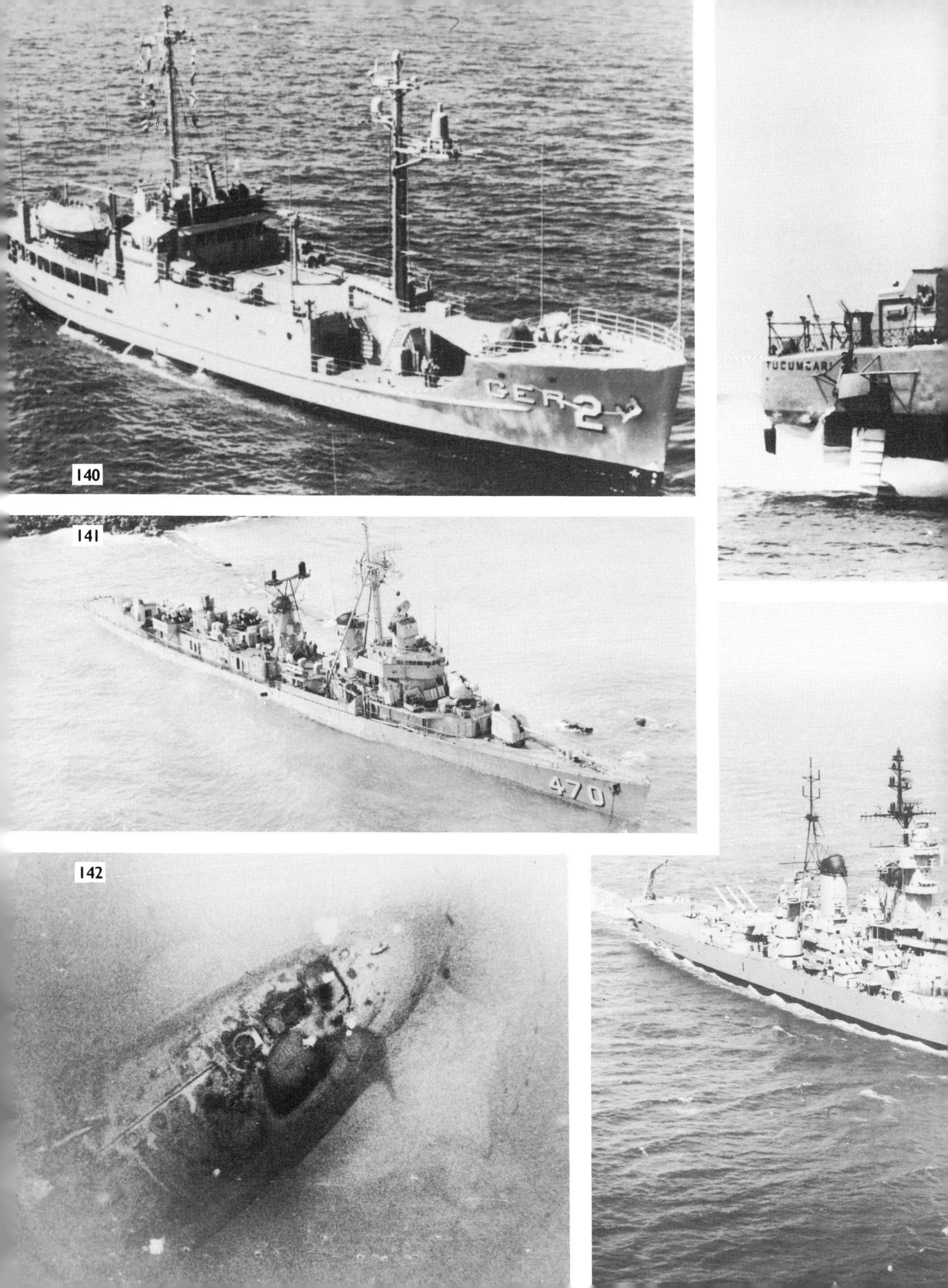

140
CER 2
TUCUMCARI
141
470
142

1968

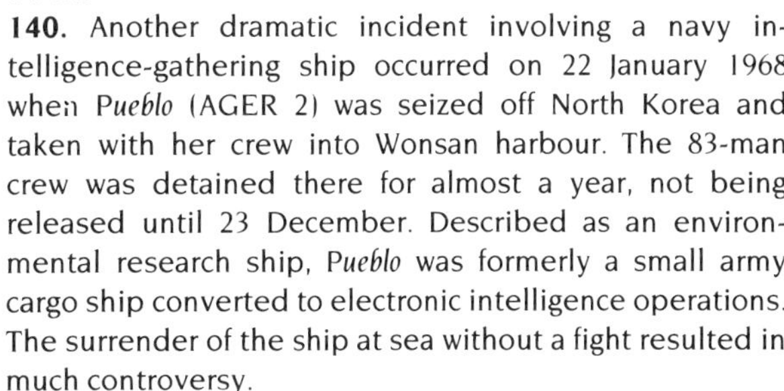

140. Another dramatic incident involving a navy intelligence-gathering ship occurred on 22 January 1968 when *Pueblo* (AGER 2) was seized off North Korea and taken with her crew into Wonsan harbour. The 83-man crew was detained there for almost a year, not being released until 23 December. Described as an environmental research ship, *Pueblo* was formerly a small army cargo ship converted to electronic intelligence operations. The surrender of the ship at sea without a fight resulted in much controversy.

141. The destroyer *Bache* (DD 470) was blown aground outside the harbour of Rhodes, Greece on 6 February 1968 by gale force winds while anchored off the island for a routine port visit. The ship was damaged beyond repair and scrapped. (KN-16237)

142. In October 1968 the wreck of the nuclear submarine *Scorpion* (SSN 589) was discovered in 10,000 feet of water 400 miles south-west of the Azores. She had been reported missing on 22 May and was declared lost with all 99 men aboard. The cause is believed to have been a torpedo explosion. This was the second loss of an American nuclear submarine. The bow section shows in this view. (USN 1136658)

143

144

143. The experimental hydrofoil gunboat programme resulted in the construction in 1967 of two competitive vessels, *Flagstaff* and *Tucumcari*. Powered by different gas turbines, they were rated at 52 knots. *Tucumcari* (PGH 2), shown here foilborne, served off Vietnam for six months during 1970. She was severely damaged when she ran aground off Puerto Rico in November 1972 and was decommissioned. *Flagstaff* served with the Coast Guard briefly in 1976 and was sold in 1978.

144. The battleship *New Jersey* (BB 62) was refitted and recommissioned on 6 April 1968 for service in Vietnam. Her three sisters had defects: *Missouri*'s speed was limited by her 1950 grounding, *Wisconsin* had damage to electric circuits from a 1958 fire, and *Iowa*'s electronics were out of date. All small anti-aircraft guns under 5in were removed and additional electronic equipment was added to the forward tower. The reduction in her complement to 1,626 officers and men was made possible by the reduction in armament. When she was decommissioned again in December 1969, after serving two tours of duty in Vietnam, it was said that no battleship would put to sea again. But that was not to be the case.

145. Commissioned in 1968, the carrier *John F. Kennedy* (CVA 67) was the last carrier built with conventional turbines. Her construction was delayed pending the decision as to whether she would be nuclear-powered. The last of the *Kitty Hawk* class, she can be distinguished by her unusual stack which is angled out to starboard. Sea Sparrow launchers can be seen on sponsons alongside the flight deck in this 1976 view.

146. *Charleston* (LKA 113) was one of five new amphibious cargo ships built in 1966–70. Each has a helicopter deck aft, and can carry nine LCM as deck cargo.

147. The repair ship *Tutuila* (ARG 4) with service craft and a Vietnamese LST alongside off Vietnam in 1967.

1969

148. Of the many craft acquired for riverine operations, the Swift boats are the most famous. Adapted from commercial boats designed to support offshore drilling rigs, they were very useful in Vietnam. There were two types with similar characteristics but different appearance of which about 125 were built. Most were used in Vietnam. This is *PCF-43* on patrol in the Cua Lon River in 1969.

149. *PCF-71* returns to base with an underwater demolition team on board in the Cua Lon River, July 1969.

150. The nuclear carrier *Enterprise* (CVAN 65) was damaged by fire and explosions on 14 January 1969 when the exhaust of a tractor accidentally set off a Zuni rocket on an aircraft waiting to be launched. The explosion triggered other rockets and bombs causing a devastating fire in the stern area of the flight deck. Twenty-seven men were killed and fifteen aircraft were destroyed. Wreckage of burned aircraft remains on the deck and a large hole is evident near the stern edge. Sea Sparrow SAM launchers can be seen on each side of the flight deck near the stern. (KN-17548)

151. While participating in a Southeast Asia Treaty Organization training exercise in the South China Sea on 2 June 1969, the destroyer *Frank E. Evans* (DD 754) was cut in two during a collision with the Australian carrier *Melbourne*. The bow section sank almost immediately and 74 men were lost. The stern section (above) remained afloat and was sunk as a target in October. (USN 1140304)

152. The navy participated in the space programme by retrieving space modules when they returned to earth at sea. Here the carrier *Hornet* (CVS 12) approaches the Apollo Twelve module after splashdown off Samoa, 24 November 1969. Navy frogmen are standing on the outside. (USN K-80888)

153. *Narwhal* (SSN 671), completed in 1969, was designed to evaluate a quieter S5G nuclear reactor. Her other characteristics are similar to the earlier *Sturgeon* class with Harpoon SSM. She is to be fitted for longer-range Tomahawk missiles.

154. A new class of escorts was commenced starting in 1964. Forty-six ships of the *Knox* class were built of which *Pharris* (DE 1094) here is a typical unit. Larger than a Second World War destroyer, they were armed with a single 5in gun and ASROC launcher forward, and a helicopter hangar aft to accommodate the DASH program. When DASH was cancelled the hangar was modified to operate LAMPS. The large 'Mack' (mast/stack) amidships gives them a distinctive appearance.

155. After 1979, the forecastle was raised to improve seakeeping as seen here in *Ainsworth* (FF 1090). The *Knox*-class ships were criticized for their single propeller and inferior armament, but the ASROC launcher was modified to launch Harpoon SSM. In the late 1980s a single Phalanx CIWS was added at the stern. Five similar vessels fitted with Tartar were built in Spain.

150

151

152

153

154

155

156

157

158

156. The submarine *Tigrone* (AGSS 419) presents an unusual appearance in her role as experimental testing ship during the late 1960s. Sonar equipment makes the bow prominent, and the conning tower has been cut down.

1970

157. Two new amphibious command ships were built in 1968–71 to replace the war-built merchant conversions. *Blue Ridge* (LCC 19) was a large purpose-built ship with hull and propulsion similar to the *Iwo Jima*-class assault ships. They were 680 feet long, with open flat decks to accommodate the many antennae used for communications. Sea Sparrow BPDMS launchers (box launcher amidships) were added in 1974.

158. The *Newport*-class tank landing ships represent a radical departure from traditional LST design, eliminating the usual bow doors to permit a pointed bow which in turn allows a higher speed. Bow and stern landing ramps permit unloading tanks and other vehicles directly on to a beach. The bow ramp is positioned on the deck behind the protruding derricks. Twenty units of this class, such as *Manitowoc* (LST 1180), were built between 1966 and 1972. They can carry 386 troops plus 500 tons of vehicles.

1973

159. The submarine rescue vessel *Ortolan* (ASR 22) was one of two built in 1969. They are the largest catamaran ships in the navy, designed with twin hulls in order to operate deep submergence rescue vehicles (DSRV). Notice the DSRV aft of the starboard funnel and the four mooring buoys mounted in the bows.

1974

160. In order to evaluate quieter machinery, a nuclear submarine was designed utilizing turbo-electric drive, which sacrificed speed for noise reduction. *Glenard P. Lipscomb* (SSN 685), launched in 1973, was larger than most previous nuclear submarines. However, the decision was made to favour speed and the succeeding *Los Angeles* class were equipped with steam turbines. Behind *Lipscomb*, in the foreground, is the first nuclear submarine, *Nautilus*.

161

164

162
37

165

163

166

1975

161. To build the 31 ships of the *Spruance* class, a new shipyard was established at Pascagoula by Ingalls Shipbuilding Division of Litton Industries. All were built at a single shipyard to utilize efficiencies of mass production. They were intended as general-purpose ships to replace the classes built during the Second World War. Here are the first six in various stages of fitting out in May 1975 (left to right): *Paul F. Foster* (DD 964), *Spruance* (963), *Arthur W. Radford* (968), *Elliot* (967), *Hewitt* (966) and *Kinkaid* (965). (USN 1162174)

162. *South Carolina* (DLGN 37) was built in 1972 as a frigate, but this classification was changed to cruiser (CGN 37) in 1975. Designed as escorts for nuclear carrier task forces, she and her sister *California* were the next nuclear-powered combatants after *Bainbridge* and *Truxtun*. Despite their large size they carried only two single launchers for Tartar or Standard missiles, an ASROC launcher and two 5in guns. There is space for a helicopter to land but no hangar.

163. Refugees in small boats from the Phan Rang area of South Vietnam come alongside the cargo ship *Durham* (LKA 114) during evacuation operations, 3 April 1975. *Durham* transported more than 3,000 refugees to safety in the south.

164. *Nimitz* (CVN 68) was commissioned in 1975, seven years after her keel was laid, having been delayed by labour problems. She is the first of a class of six nuclear carriers, the largest warships ever built. They can operate about 90 aircraft and have a maximum capacity of 2.7 million gallons of aviation fuel. Sea Sparrow SSM launchers can be seen forward and aft.

165. The fire-ravaged hull of the cruiser *Belknap* (CG 26) under tow to Naples. Notice the crew members standing on the deck aft. She was severely damaged in a collision with the carrier *John F. Kennedy* and the resulting fire while on night manoeuvres in the Ionian Sea on 22 November 1975. Despite the extensive damage she was repaired and rebuilt and was recommissioned in May 1980.

166. *LCU-1643*, with about 300 American citizens on board, approaches the open well of the landing ship *Coronado* (LPD 11) off Beirut, Lebanon, 27 July 1976. Americans were evacuated because of the civil war in that country.

167

168

1976

167. *Tarawa* (LHA 1) was the lead ship of a new class of amphibious assault ships which were the largest warships built apart from aircraft carriers. Displacing 39,300 tons full load with a length of 820 feet, they are in fact large helicopter carriers, able to carry about 30 helicopters and 1,900 troops. They also have a docking well in the stern (open in the picture) which can hold four LCU. Nine were planned but only five were built between 1971 and 1980. One of her two Sea Sparrow BPDMS launchers is visible at the stern.

168. *Mississippi* (CGN 40) was the third ship of four of the *Virginia* class, the last class of nuclear cruisers. They were built at Newport News between 1972 and 1980, construction having been delayed by disagreements with the shipyard. Improved *California*s they mounted a new missile-launcher capable of handling three different

169

170

missile types. In 1984–8 the helicopter hangar in the stern was replaced with 2 quad Tomahawk missile canisters.

169. LCU heading towards docking well of *Saipan* (LHA 2) while a Sea Knight helicopter takes off.

170. O'*Brien* (DD 975) is typical of the *Spruance* class, the first US surface combatants with gas-turbine propulsion. They were designed for modular replacement of weapon systems. The funnels are off-centre to port and starboard. The class was originally designed without a SAM system but Harpoon and Tomahawk have been added to all units.

171. The submarine *New York City* (SSN 696) travelling at speed on the surface in 1978. The standard attack submarine developed in the 1960s resulted in the *Los Angeles* class which has been in series production since 1970. A total of sixty-four units are planned through 1989, all being built by either General Dynamics at Groton, Connecticut or Newport News in Virginia. These submarines have four 21in torpedo tubes and are equipped to launch Tomahawk, Harpoon and Subroc missiles. They have a larger reactor than previous classes in order to obtain 5 knots additional speed, and are the fastest and quietest American submarines. Earlier units are being retrofitted with vertical launch tubes for Tomahawk cruise missiles. Submarines no longer have their numbers painted on.

171

172

173

174

175

1977

172. In 1973 six hydrofoil missile boats were ordered but only one, *Pegasus* (PHM 1), was completed. Originally a programme of 30 boats, the other five were cancelled in 1977, but reordered several months later after Congress refused to rescind its authorization. All were completed by 1982 and were armed with four single Harpoon launchers which were later replaced by two quad launchers aft as in *Pegasus*, above. Foilborne they can travel in excesss of 48 knots.

173. Requiring ocean escorts for merchant convoys, replenishment groups and amphibious forces, the navy designed the frigates of the *Oliver Hazard Perry* class, starting construction in 1974. *Clark* (FFG 11) is shown in April 1989 (note absence of Phalanx). Fifty-one ships were built, the largest class of destroyer types built in the West since the Second World War. There is a single launcher for Standard and Harpoon missiles forward and a 3in gun amidships. A Phalanx CIWS was fitted in most active ships during the 1980s. *Stark* and *Samuel B. Roberts* of this class were damaged in the Persian Gulf in 1987–8.

176

174. The guided-missile frigate *Thach* (FFG 43) during sea trials off California in October 1984. She was completed with her Phalanx CIWS gatling gun aft (white dome). Four additional units of the *Perry* class were built for Australia.

1981

175. *Scott* (DDG 995), shown in 1986 in the Mediterranean, is one of four ships of the *Kidd* class, similar to the *Spruance* class with increased anti-aircraft and anti-submarine capability. Originally a class of six ordered for Iran, four were taken over by the US Navy while under construction. They are named for admirals who died during the Second World War, and *Scott* commemorates Rear Admiral Norman Scott, killed in action on board the cruiser *San Francisco* during the Battle of Guadalcanal. Harpoon SSM and Phalanx CIWS were added after completion.

176. The lead-ship of the Trident submarine programme, *Ohio* (SSBN 726) at sea on her first sea trials in September 1981. These ships are the largest submarines yet built in the United States, with the sail mounted far forward on the 560ft-long hull. The Trident C-4 missiles are housed in 24 tubes aft of the sail. Later ships of the class carry the D-5 missile with a greater range (about 6,000 miles), heavier payload and more accurate targeting than the C-4. *Ohio*-class submarines are reported to have an operating depth of 1,000 feet. They operate on 70-day patrols with two crews (blue and gold) alternating during 25-day overhaul periods.

177

1983

177. Phalanx CIWS was added to the *Spruance* class in the late 1980s. *Caron* (DD 970) has one on the forward superstructure, the other is situated amidships next to the second funnel on the port side. A 61-cell VLS system is being fitted in 24 ships of the class replacing the ASROC launcher. *Spruance* was the first to be converted in 1988.

178. *Ticonderoga* (CG 47), completed in 1983, is the lead-ship of the newest cruiser class, carrying the controversial AEGIS radar system, designed automatically to detect, track and attack multiple targets. The efficacy of AEGIS, marked by the panels on the superstructure, was sorely tried when *Vincennes* destroyed an Iranian airliner by mistake in the Persian Gulf in 1988. Later units have vertical launching tubes for Tomahawk, Standard and ASROC missiles in place of the launchers in *Ticonderoga*. These cruisers were designed to provide defence for carrier battle groups against aircraft and anti-ship missiles.

1984

179. A new class of ocean surveillance ships was commenced in 1982 to provide for additional detection of submarines. Sixteen ships like *Stalwart* (T-AGOS 1) were built. Civilian-manned, they operate SURTASS (Surveil-

179

lance Towed Array Sensor System) which is to supplement SOSUS (Sound Surveillance System) on the seafloor in areas where SOSUS is inadequate. SOSUS is a surveillance system on the seafloor, while SURTASS is a submarine detection system towed by ships.

180. The newly recommissioned *Iowa* (BB 61) firing all nine 16in guns at once while exercising near Vieques Island on 1 July 1984. Amidships around the second funnel can be seen the eight box launchers for Tomahawk missiles and the smaller canister launchers for Harpoon. In April 1989 she suffered an explosion in number two turret which wiped out the gun crew.

181. After the Iranian revolution and the seizure of the American embassy in Teheran, a Rapid Deployment Force was set up and a variety of ships was acquired. Some are loaded with weapons and supplies and stationed in readiness (pre-positioned) in the Indian Ocean. Others are laid up in readiness for rapid loading in American ports. The cargo ship *Antares* (T-AKR 294) is one of eight former merchant ships built in 1971–3 and converted in 1984–6 to Fast Sealift Ships with extensive Roll-on/Roll-off capability. They are not pre-positioned but kept in Atlantic ports ready rapidly to load military equipment.

1986

182. The battleship *Iowa* inches her way through the Pedro Miguel Locks of the Panama Canal in February 1986. Her beam of 108 feet 2 inches leaves less than one foot to spare on each side. The aircraft carrier *Midway* of 1945 was the first US warship built too wide to pass through the canal. The massive 16in gun turrets are hidden by the sheer of the bow, but the 5in turrets on each beam are visible as are the white domes of two Phalanx guns.

183. The two Phalanx guns high up on her superstructure are the only defensive weapons on the dock landing ship *Germantown* (LSD 42). There is a large helicopter landing area aft but no hangar. About 500 troops can be carried by ships of this class. They are the first US ships powered with medium-speed diesel engines. This view was taken on her trials in October 1985 prior to commissioning.

184. The fast combat support ship *Seattle* (AOE 3) engaged in under way replenishment with the carrier *Saratoga* in the Mediterranean in 1986. She has a Sea Sparrow launcher forward and one of her two new Phalanx guns is visible aft by the funnel. Four more of this class are planned for completion before 1994.

1987

185. The amphibious assault ship *Wasp* (LHD 1) just prior

182

183

184

185

186

to her launching at Ingalls in July 1987. The ship was moved 276 feet to the water's edge becoming the world's heaviest man-made object to be moved over land. The stern docking well is open and the starboard deck-edge elevator aft is open. Notice the square shape of the stern and the projecting bow underwater. Originally planned to be smaller than the previous *Tarawa* class, they are actually somewhat larger partly in order to accommodate more Harrier VSTOL aircraft. *Wasp* was commissioned in 1989.

186. The aircraft carrier *Theodore Roosevelt* (CVN 71) at sea with the fleet in September 1988. A Sea Knight helicopter hovers overhead delivering ammunition from the carrier *Forrestal*. The fourth unit of the *Nimitz* class, she took five years to build, being commissioned in 1986. Newport News is the only American shipyard able to build these huge ships.

187. Looking down on the stern of *Theodore Roosevelt*, a variety of aircraft are parked on the flight deck. Poised on the port side catapult is a F-14A Tomcat and others wait on the stern. Notice the blast protecter immediately behind the aircraft. On the stern are two white-topped Phalanx guns and at flight deck level can be seen two NATO Sea Sparrow launchers.

188

188. *Avenger* (MCM 1), lead-ship of a new class of mine countermeasures ships, was completed in September 1987. Laid down in 1982, her completion was two years behind schedule, delayed by improperly installed engines. Fourteen are building or planned up to 1991. The hull is constructed of fibreglass-sheathed wood. No guns are carried.

1988

189. The hospital ship *Comfort* (T-AH 20) and her sister *Mercy* were converted from tankers to support the pre-positioning forces. They are 894 feet long and have beds for more than 1,000 patients. It is anticipated that most patients would be brought on board by helicopter. *Comfort* is shown undergoing sea trials in October 1987.

189